# Computer Accounting Essentials using QuickBooks: Online Edition

## Second Edition

Carol Yacht, MA
*Software Consultant*

Susan V. Crosson, MS
*Professor of Accounting*
*Santa Fe Community College*

**McGraw-Hill Irwin**

Boston   Burr Ridge, IL   Dubuque, IA   Madison, WI   New York   San Francisco   St. Louis
Bangkok   Bogotá   Caracas   Kuala Lumpur   Lisbon   London   Madrid   Mexico City
Milan   Montreal   New Delhi   Santiago   Seoul   Singapore   Sydney   Taipei   Toronto

McGraw-Hill
Irwin

COMPUTER ACCOUNTING ESSENTIALS USING QUICKBOOKS: ONLINE
EDITION
Carol Yacht, M. A. and Susan V. Crosson

Published by McGraw-Hill/Irwin, an imprint of The McGraw-Hill Companies, Inc., 1221
Avenue of the Americas, New York, NY 10020. Copyright © 2005, 2004 by The
McGraw-Hill Companies, Inc. All rights reserved.

1 2 3 4 5 6 7 8 9 0 QPD/QPD 0 9 8 7 6 5 4
ISBN 0-07-286659-4

Vice president and editor-in-chief: *Robin Zwettler*
Editorial director: *Brent Gordon*
Publisher: *Stewart Mattson*
Sponsoring editor: *Steve Schuetz*
Developmental editor: *Jennifer Jelinski*
Senior supplement producer: *Susan Lombardi*
Production supervisor: *Debra Sylvester*
Cover designer: *Kami Carter*
Marketing manager: *Katherine Mattison*
Media producer: *Gregory Bates*

www.mhhe.com

*About the Authors*

**Carol Yacht** is a textbook author and educator. Carol contributes regularly to professional journals and is the author of Peachtree, QuickBooks, and Excel textbooks. She started teaching computer accounting in 1978. Carol's teaching career includes Yavapai College; West Los Angeles Community College; California State University, Los Angeles; and Beverly Hills High School and Adult School. Carol is the editor of the *Communicator*, the American Accounting Association's two-year college section publication and an officer of that section. She worked for IBM Corporation as an education instruction specialist, and served on the Computer Education Task Force for the National Business Education Association. Carol is a frequent speaker at state, regional, and national conventions; technical school consortium meetings; and Department of Education conferences. She earned her AS degree from Temple University, BS degree from the University of New Mexico, and MA degree from California State University, Los Angeles.

**Susan V. Crosson** is Professor and Accounting Faculty Coordinator at Santa Fe Community College, Gainesville, FL. With more than twenty years teaching experience at Santa Fe Community College, University of Florida, Washington University in St. Louis, University of Oklahoma, Johnson County Community College in Kansas, and Kansas City Kansas Community College, Susan is known for her innovative application of pedagogical strategies online and in the classroom. She is a recipient of an Institute of Management Accountants' Faculty Development Grant to blend technology into the classroom, the Florida Association of Community Colleges Professor of the Year Award for Instructional Excellence, and the University of Oklahoma's Halliburton Education Award for Excellence. Susan is active in many academic and professional organizations. She serves on the Florida Association of Accounting Educators Steering Committee and is slated to become Vice President of Sections and Regions for the American Accounting Association. She has previously served as Two-Year Accounting Section Chair, Membership Committee Chair, and as a Council Member at Large for the American Accounting Association. In addition, she has chaired the Florida Institute of CPAs Relations with Accounting Educators Committee. Susan holds a BBA in Economics and Accounting from Southern Methodist University and a MS in Accounting from Texas Tech University. She is a certified public accountant in the state of Texas.

# Preface

*Computer Accounting Essentials Using QuickBooks: Online Edition* teaches you how to use the Internet-based accounting program QuickBooks: Online Edition. In this book, you will sign up for a free trial of QuickBooks: Online Edition. Then, you will start a service business from scratch and enter all the business transactions for the service business. The activities will take about 25 hours to complete. Try to set aside those 25 hours within the free trial period. If you decide to extend QuickBooks: Online Edition beyond the free trial, there is a monthly subscription fee (at time of printing, $19.95/month).

QuickBooks: Online Edition is designed for service-based businesses with broadband connections. Although new features are continually being added to QuickBooks: Online Edition; to obtain additional features like pay bills online, online banking, track purchase orders and inventory, create a forecast, and track sales orders; the desktop version of QuickBooks software must be purchased and installed.

## Browser Requirements

If you can access QuickBooks: Online Edition's web site at http://www.oe.quickbooks.com you already have what is needed – a computer, a browser, and a modem. QuickBooks: Online Edition is an operating system that works with Windows 98, XP, or 2000. Mac OS is not supported. Continuous high-speed Internet access using DSL, cable modem, or T1 is recommended. QuickBooks: Online Edition does work using any Internet access, although processing time can be slow. It prefers the browser version 6 or higher of Internet Explorer® on Windows.[1]

---

[1] For more system requirement details, access the link to QuickBooks: Online Edition's home page at www.oe.quickbooks.com

---

*Computer Accounting Essentials Using QuickBooks: Online Edition* has six parts:

1. Downloading QuickBooks: Online Edition

2. New Company Setup

3. Setting Accounting Defaults

4. Fourth-Quarter Transactions

5. End-of-Year & Beginning-of-Year Transactions

6. Advanced Features

Each part of *Computer Accounting Essentials Using QuickBooks: Online Edition* includes:

➢ Software objectives

➢ Web objectives

➢ Step-by-step instructions with screen captures

➢ Transactions and reports

➢ Check your progress

➢ Internet homework

➢ Multiple-choice

➢ True/false

➢ End-of-part exercises

In *Computer Accounting Essentials Using QuickBooks: Online Edition* you learn how to set up a service business. When you finish this book, you will have a working familiarity with QuickBooks: Online Edition, a web-based accounting program.

Text and screen variations may occur since web-based software products backup and upgrade automatically.

**Part 1:  Downloading QuickBooks:  Online Edition**

In Part 1, you will download QuickBooks:  Online Edition software from the Internet.  The step-by-step instructions show you how to do that.

**Part 2:  New Company Setup**

In Part 2, you will learn how to use the software to set up a service business.
New Company Setup includes selecting a chart of accounts, entering opening balances, and printing a beginning balance sheet.

**Part 3:  Setting Accounting Defaults**

In Part 3, you learn how to set defaults for accounts payable, accounts receivable, and cash transactions that follow in Part 4.  Defaults are information or commands that the software automatically uses.  You also learn how to change default settings.

**Part 4:  Fourth-Quarter Transactions**

In Part 4, you record transactions for the fourth quarter of the year:  October, November and December.  You will record accounts payable, accounts receivable, and cash transactions.  At the end of each month's transactions, you will reconcile the bank statement.

**Part 5:  End-of-Year & Beginning-of-Year Transactions**

In Part 5, you will complete end-of-year adjusting entries, print financial statements, and make closing entries.  Part 5 also includes transactions for the start of the new year – January 1 - 31, 20XX.

**Part 6:  Advanced Features**

In Part 6, you learn how to memorize forms, customize forms, copy data to Microsoft Excel and create graphs, and print your activity log.

## Case Problem 1

Case Problem 1 includes two more months of transactions for your service business – February and March.  You will complete the accounting cycle for the first quarter and print reports.

## Case Problem 2

Case Problem 2 includes the end-of-quarter transactions for the first quarter.  You will complete the accounting cycle for the first quarter and print reports.

## Case Problem 3

Case Problem 3 is a student-designed project.  You are instructed to write transactions for the next month and complete the accounting cycle showing a net loss for your business.

**Glossary:**  Terms that are boldfaced and italicized through the book appear here.

**Index:**  The introduction and each part of the book ends with an index. The index at the end of the book is an alphabetic listing of these individual indexes.

# Table of Contents

| TIMETABLE FOR COMPLETION | | Hours |
|---|---|---|
| Part 1 | Downloading QuickBooks: Online Edition | 1.0 |
| Part 2 | New Company Setup | 1.5 |
| Part 3 | Setting Accounting Defaults | 3.0 |
| Part 4 | Fourth-Quarter Transactions | 6.0 |
| Part 5 | End-of-Year & Beginning-of-Year Transactions | 4.0 |
| Part 6 | Advanced Features | 2.0 |
| Case Problem 1 | Complete First Quarter Transactions | 2.5 |
| Case Problem 2 | End-of-Quarter Adjusting Entries and Reports | 1.5 |
| Case Problem 3 | Student-Designed Project | 2.0 |
| Final Exam | | 1.5 |
| | TOTAL HOURS | 25.0 |

Text and screen variations may occur since web-based software products backup and upgrade automatically.

# Introduction

*Computer Accounting Essentials Using QuickBooks: Online Edition* teaches you how to use QuickBooks: Online Edition, a popular online accounting package for small business. From any computer connected to the *Internet* QuickBooks: Online Edition users can work on their business's finances anytime, anywhere. Owners, employees, financial advisors, and accountants can work simultaneously in different locations.

To use QuickBooks: Online Edition, you need a connection to the Internet and a *browser*. A browser is the software used on a computer to connect and display information from a Web site called a server. Commonly used web browsers are Internet Explorer® and Netscape Navigator®.

The Internet is the worldwide electronic communication network that allows for the sharing of information. The Internet is also called the World Wide Web (WWW) or Web.

QuickBooks: Online Edition works on computers with Windows 98, ME, NT, XP, or 2000. Mac OS is not supported. It uses the browser version 5 or above of Internet Explorer® for an Internet connection to QuickBooks: Online Edition.

To make an Internet connection, your computer must be equipped with a *modem*. The word modem is an abbreviation of **Mo**dulator/**Dem**odulator. A modem is a device that translates the digital signals from your computer into analog signals that can travel over telephone lines.

Once you set up your modem to dial the appropriate phone number to an *Internet Service Provider* (ISP), you can connect to the Internet. ISPs can be companies such as America OnLine™ (AOL), CompuServe™, Earthlink™, or local providers. Because telephone lines were designed for voice communication, not electronic data from a computer, modem connections via telephone lines are usually slow.

Faster connections to the Internet are possible using *an **Integrated Services Digital Network*** (ISDN) or leased lines.  An ISDN line is a digital network that provides faster transmission of voice, video, and text.  Leased lines, referred to as T-1 and T-3, are available for faster connections, too.  The backbone of the Internet consists of T-3 lines.  Leased lines are expensive and used by companies that need to transfer massive amounts of data.

Faster Internet connections are also being offered via cable, wireless radio modems, and satellite TV.  A digital subscriber line (DSL) is another way to access the Internet faster.  DSL lines are always connected to the Internet  (are always *on*) so there is no need to dial up. Continuous high-speed Internet access using DSL, cable modem, or T1 is recommended when using QuickBooks:  Online Edition.

In the next section, Downloading QuickBooks:  Online Edition, you will learn how to go to QuickBooks:  Online Edition's web site at www.oe.quickbooks.com.  You will also start using QuickBooks:  Online Edition to record business transactions.

## INDEX

# 1 Downloading QuickBooks: Online Edition

In Part 1 of *Computer Accounting Essentials Using QuickBooks: Online Edition*, you will set up the QuickBooks: Online Edition (formerly known as QuickBooks for the Web) software on the Internet.  The step-by-step instructions that follow show you how to do this.

**SOFTWARE OBJECTIVES:  In Part 1, you use the software to:**

1. Start QuickBooks: Online Edition.
2. Sign up for free 30-day trial version of QuickBooks: Online Edition.
3. Give your company a unique name.
4. Select "Miscellaneous services" as the company type.
5. Assign a password.
6. Confirm signup information.
7. Complete activities for Part 1, Downloading QuickBooks: Online Edition.

**WEB OBJECTIVES:  In Part 1, you use the Internet to:**

1. Access the Computer Accounting Essentials web site at www.mhhe.com/yachtessentials2e to check for updates.
2. Access QuickBooks: Online Edition's web site at http://oe.quickbooks.com.
3. Download QuickBooks: Online Edition's 30-day free trial version.
4. Log in to your QuickBooks: Online Edition account.
5. Receive an email from QuickBooks.
6. Log off from QuickBooks: Online Edition.
7. Complete Internet homework.

## COMPUTER ACCOUNTING ESSENTIALS WEB SITE

Before you begin your work in Part 1, Downloading QuickBooks: Online Edition, access the Computer Accounting Essentials web site at www.mhhe.com/yachtessentials2e. Select the QuickBooks link, and then link to Text Updates.  Check this web site regularly for reference and study.

---

## GETTING STARTED

Follow these steps to download QuickBooks: Online Edition.

1.  Start your Internet browser.  You need Version 5 or higher of Microsoft Internet Explorer for an Internet connection to QuickBooks: Online Edition.

> **Comment:**
> Internet Explorer, Version 6 was used for the screen illustrations shown in *Computer Accounting Essentials using QuickBooks: Online Edition.*

2.  Explore QuickBooks: Online Edition's website

    a.  Go to http://oe.quickbooks.com. The "QuickBooks: Online Edition" screen appears.
    b.  Click on the [➋ **Pricing**] link. The "Pricing" screen appears.

    Read the information on this screen. Review the information in the "Your Online Edition subscription includes" section.
    c.  Click on the [➋ **Features**] link. The "Features" screen appears. Scroll down the screen to review QuickBooks: Online Edition features.

        ➤    Bill customers
        ➤    Pay bills
        ➤    Gain more control over your business finances
        ➤    Work smart by working online
        ➤    Track your accounts
        ➤    Manage employees and contractors
        ➤    Import and export financial data
        ➤    Get started quickly and easily
        ➤    Plus Package Features
        ➤    Upcoming Online Edition features
        ➤    Features not yet available in QuickBooks: Online Edition

    d.  If necessary, scroll up the screen. Then, click on the [➋ **Compare**] link.  The "Compare" screen appears.  Scroll down the chart to see a comparison with other QuickBooks products.

e. Click on the [Online Security] link. The "Online Security" screen appears. Read the information on this screen.

f. Click on the [Fits Your Business] link. The "Fits Your Business" screen appears. Read the information on this screen.

g. Click on the [Support] link. The "Support" screen appears. Read the information on this screen.

3. Download the 30-day Free Trial Version of QuickBooks: Online Edition.

a. The "QuickBooks: Online Edition" screen should be displayed. If not, go to http://oe.quickbooks.com.

b. Click on [Try it for free]

c. Link to [Start with Your Data]

d. The "QuickBooks: Online Edition Startup Interview" screen appears. Click on the radio button next to "I am new to QuickBooks Business Services." A form appears. Instructions for completing this form are shown below.

> **Comment**
> Some interview question variation may exist between this text and the interview you complete since QuickBooks continuously upgrades its software to better serve its users.

e. Answer the following questions for new users. (Press the <Tab> key between fields.)

1. **What is your name?** Type your first and last name.

2. **Enter an email address to receive your password confirmation.** Type your email address; type your email address again. *Write your email address on the line below.*

_____

3. **What would you like your login name to be?** (*Your email address shows up in this box. It is okay to use your email address as your login name.*)

   If necessary, type your 4-40 character case-sensitive name.

   *Write your Login Name here:*

   _defourd www.login@BOE.com_

4. **What would you like your password to be?** Type a 6-12 character password that contains letters or numbers but no spaces.

   *Write your password here:*

   _Candy5_

   Type *exactly* the same password again.

5. **What would you like your password hint to be?** Type a password hint that will be asked if you forget your password.

   *Write your password hint here:*

   _Sweet_

6. **What would you like your challenge question to be?** Select a challenge question that will be asked if you forget your password.

   *Write your challenge question here:*

   _____

7. **What is the answer to the challenge question?** Type the answer to your challenge question.

   *Write your answer here:*

   _____

Text and screen variations may occur since web-based software products backup and upgrade automatically.

f.   Answer No to the "Import data" question asking

>   **Do you want to start with data from another version of QuickBooks?**

g.   Click on **Next**. The "QuickBooks: Online Edition Startup Interview" screen appears.

In the section that follows, you will complete information on the "Customize QuickBooks: Online Edition" form. Follow these directions carefully because your responses will be used in Part 2, New Company Setup.

## 1. Company Information

   a.  **What is the name of your business?** Type **XXXXXXX Service Corporation** (the X's indicate your first and last name); for example; Susan Crosson Service Corporation (use your first and last name). In this book, XXXXX Service Corporation will be used for the company name. You should use your first and last name so that report printouts have your name on them.

   b.  **What is the email address of your business?** If necessary, type your email account again.

   c.  **What's your business address?** Type your address; type your city; select your state; type your Zip code; type your phone number [optional].

## 2.  What type of business do you have?

   a.  **Please select an industry:** In the menu scroll to "Miscellaneous services" and then select "All Other Miscellaneous Services."

   b.  **Please select the role you play in the business:** From the menu, select "Owner/Partner/CEO."

## 3.  How is this business conducted? Select "One or more shareholders" (A corporation)  "Tax Form 1120"

4. **What does your business call the people who give you money?** Select "Customers." Compare your screen to the one shown.

**2. What type of business do you have?**

Knowing your industry helps us set up the right accounts for your business.

**Please select an industry:**

All Other Miscellaneous Services ⌄

**Please select the role you play in this business:**

Owner/Partner/CEO ⌄

**3. How is this business conducted?**

This information helps us set up the right accounts.

○ One owner (A sole proprietor)          Tax Form 1040
○ Two or more owners (A partnership or limited liability company)    Tax Form 1065
○ One or more shareholders (A small business corporation)    Tax Form 1120S
◉ One or more shareholders (A corporation)    Tax Form 1120
○ Non profit    Tax Form 990
○ Other/None

**4. What does your business call the people who give you money?**

For example, if you are a doctor, select Patients. The term you select will be used throughout QuickBooks Online Edition when you log in. You can change this terminology later from within the product.

○ Clients
◉ Customers
○ Donors
○ Guests
○ Members
○ Patients
○ Tenants

g. Click on **Next**. The "Finish setup" screen appears. Answer the questions using the following information.

1. **Do you want help setting up your accounts?** If necessary, select "Yes."

   a. **Do you have any loans your business owes?** Select "No."

   b. **Do you have any outstanding loans owed to your business?** Select "No."

   c. **Do you have employees?** Select "No." Compare your screen to the one shown on the next page.

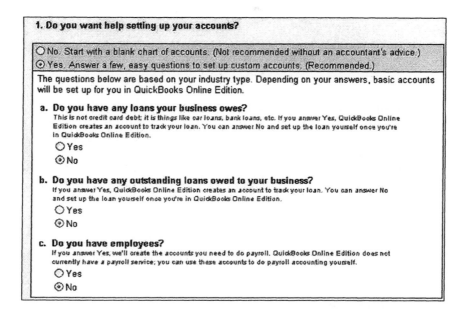

2. **Where did you hear about QuickBooks: Online Edition?** Select "Other."

3. **May we contact you?** Skip this section, or make appropriate selections.

4. **User Agreement:** I accept

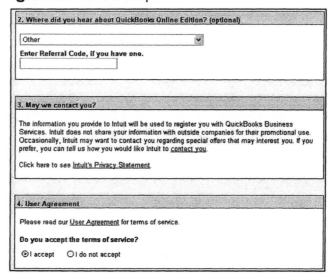

---

> **Comment**
> The information you have entered will not be saved until you click the "Start Free Trial…" button in step h.

h. Review your "Summary" information. Then, click on `Next`. A screen pops up saying that your company is being created. When the "→Start Free Trial Now" screen appears, click on `Start Free Trial..`. The "Congratulations!" screen tells you that your free trial of QuickBooks: Online Edition has now begun. Read the information on this screen.

> **IMPORTANT!** Student use of the 30 day free trial DOES NOT include support. **DO NOT contact QuickBooks with questions!**
> The following **DOES NOT APPLY TO YOU….**
>
> **Click support from any page to submit a question.**
>
> ▶ Support is available M-F from 8 am to 4 pm Pacific Time.
> ▶ We will contact you within 20 minutes during business hours.

i. After reading the information on this screen, click on `Proceed to QuickBooks Online Edition`. Then, continue with step 4.

> **Comment**
> If an "ActiveX Description—Web Page Dialog" box pops up, click on "Continue." Then, when the "Security Warning" screen pops up, click on "Yes." Continue with step 4.

4. The "QuickBooks Financial Software Online Edition" home screen appears. Your business "Welcome" screen is shown. You can log back on to QB Online Edition from any Internet connection, which means you can continue your work anytime and anywhere.[1]

---

[1] You will receive an email from the QuickBooks: Online Edition Team confirming your account information. When you check your email, you can read this message. Additional information about how to log in, adding users, startup checklist, and getting help is included in this email.

---

Text and screen variations may occur since web-based software products backup and upgrade automatically.

## LOGGING OUT OF QUICKBOOKS: ONLINE EDITION

To log out of QuickBooks: Online Edition, proceed with the following steps.

1. To log off, click on the 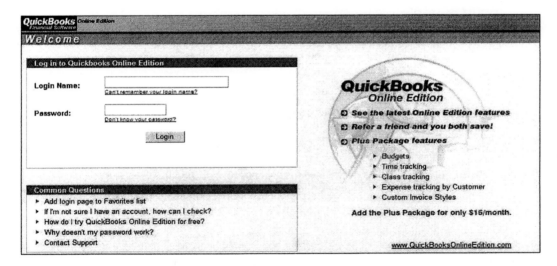 button on the top right of your screen.

2. You could exit at this point or continue. Since the instructions that follow assume you are logging back in, do not close your browser at this time.

## LOGGING IN TO QUICKBOOKS: ONLINE EDITION: If you did *not* exit your browser

A screen similar to the one shown below should be displayed.

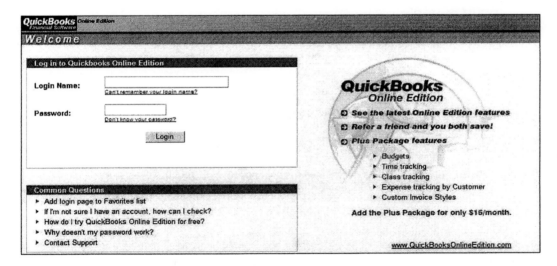

1. If necessary, complete your "Login Name."
2. Type your password. You *must* use the same login name and password that you assigned in the QuickBooks Online Interview, steps **3** (login name) and **4** (password), page 6.

3. Click [ Login ]. After a few moments your "Home" screen appears.

4. Log out, then close your browser.

**LOGGING IN TO QUICKBOOKS: ONLINE EDITION: If you logged out completely and closed your browser, follow these steps.**

1.  Check your email. You should have an email from serviceconsulting@quickbooks.com. Read the email.

2.  The subject of your email from QuickBooks is "Log in Now to QuickBooks: Online Edition!" In the How to Log in section of the email there is a link to your account. Your login name is also shown.

3.  Link to the web site shown in the email. As of this writing, it was https://accounting.quickbooks.com. That takes you to the QuickBooks: Online Edition Welcome page. Your Login name is shown.

4.  Type in your password, then click Login . You business's Home page appears.

**CHECK YOUR PROGRESS**

**Internet Homework**

1.  If you are already logged in, you do not have to start QuickBooks: Online Edition again. If necessary, go to http://oe.quickbooks.com. The "QuickBooks: Online Edition" screen appears.

    a. Click on the Features link. The "Features" screen appears. Scroll down the screen to review QuickBooks: Online Edition features.

    > Bill customers
    > Pay bills
    > Gain more control over your business finances
    > Work smart by working online
    > Track your accounts
    > Manage employees and contractors
    > Import and export financial data
    > Get started quickly and easily
    > Plus Package Features
    > Upcoming Online Edition features
    > Features not yet available in QuickBooks: Online Edition

---

Text and screen variations may occur since web-based software products backup and upgrade automatically.

b.  If necessary, scroll up the screen. Then, click on the ⊙ **Compare** link.  The "Compare" screen appears.  Scroll down the chart to see a comparison with other QuickBooks products.

2.  For QuickBooks: Online Edition and one other QuickBooks product, write a 50 to 75-word essay describing each of the product's' features and compare the two products to each other.  Include the web address of each of the products.  Use a word-processing program to type your reports.  Here are a couple hints for completing your report:

a.  Spell check your report before turning it in.
b.  To use copy/paste for long web addresses, highlight the web address.  Then from the menu bar, select Edit, Copy.  From your word processing program, click on Edit, Paste.

**Multiple-Choice**:  In the space provided, write the letter that best answers each question.

_____1.  To use QuickBooks: Online Edition, you need to use the following browser:

a.  Version 5 or higher of Microsoft Internet Explorer.
b.  Microsoft Windows.
c.  Microsoft Office.
d.  None of the above.
e.  All of the above.

_____2.  To start QuickBooks: Online Edition, you type the following web address.

a.  www.microsoft.com
b.  www.yahoo.com
c.  www.QuickBooks.net
d.  www.peachtree.com
e.  None of the above.

_____3.  From QuickBooks: Online Edition's home page, you can do the following:

    a.  Sign up.
    b.  Log in.
    c.  Select links.
    d.  Learn more about QuickBooks: Online Edition.
    e.  All of the above.

_____4.  The software that you downloaded is called:

    a.  QuickBooks: Online Edition.
    b.  QuickBooks: Online Edition Business.
    c.  QuickBooks: Online Edition Personal.
    d.  QuickBooks: Online Edition Checking.
    e.  None of the above.

_____5.  When QuickBooks: Online Edition is loading, the following icon appears on your screen.

    a.  Hourglass.
    b.  Hand.
    c.  Arrow.
    d.  I-bar.
    e.  None of the above.

_____6.  How long can you use QuickBooks: Online Edition for free:

    a.  10 days.
    b.  20 days.
    c.  30 days.
    d.  40 days.
    e.  None of the above.

_____7.  You set up the following type of business with QuickBooks: Online Edition:

  a.  General.
  b.  Manufacturing.
  c.  Service.
  d.  Retail.
  e.  None of the above.

_____8.  In order to make changes to your startup interview, you use:

  a.  Submit.
  b.  Back.
  c.  Basic.
  d.  Log off.
  e.  None of the above.

_____9.  After signing up for QuickBooks: Online Edition, you receive:

  a.  Instructions displayed on your screen.
  b.  An email from QuickBooks: Online Edition.
  c.  An Authentication code from QuickBooks.
  d.  Both a. and b. are true.
  e.  None of the above.

_____10.  After signing up for QuickBooks: Online Edition, you need to use the following to log in:

  a.  Login name and password.
  b.  Authentication code.
  c.  Email address.
  d.  Name and address.
  e.  None of the above.

**True/False**: Write T for True and F for false in the space provided.

_____11.  You download QuickBooks: Online Edition software from the Internet.

_____12.  You use Outlook Express to download QuickBooks: Online Edition.

_____13.    The web address for QuickBooks: Online Edition is
        http://oe.quickbooks.com

_____14.    The software that you download is called QuickBooks: Online
        Edition Household.

_____15.    When signing up for QuickBooks: Online Edition you identify a
        challenge question and answer.

_____16.    The trial version of QuickBooks: Online Edition will last for two
        months.

_____17.    When assigning a name for your business, use the same name
        as everyone else.

_____18.    You must use your login name and password each time you
        start QuickBooks: Online Edition.

_____19.    A browser is the software used on a computer to connect to the
        Internet.

_____20.    The World Wide Web is a branch of the Internet.


**Exercise 1-1**. QuickBooks: Online Edition keeps a log of your activities
    while using the software. To print your "Activity Log," complete the
    following steps:

1. On your Company home page, move
   your mouse over "Company on the
   QuickBooks: Online Edition menu bar.
   When the drop-down menu appears,
   click on "Activity Log."
2. When the activity log appears, notice it
   displays the date, time, user, and
   activity while on your company site.
3. Click on the **Print...** to print your
   "Activity Log."
4. Click on **logout** to exit QuickBooks: Online Edition.
5. Exit your browser.

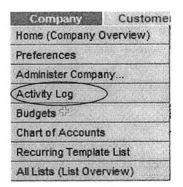

---

Text and screen variations may occur since web-based software products backup and upgrade automatically.

## PART 1 INDEX

# 2 New Company Setup

In Part 2 of *Computer Accounting Essentials Using QuickBooks: Online Edition,* you will learn how to use the software to set up your business. New Company Setup includes selecting preferences, a chart of accounts, entering opening balances for your business, and printing a beginning balance sheet.

**SOFTWARE OBJECTIVES:  In Part 2, you use the software to:**

1.  Set company preferences.
2.  Enter October as the first fiscal month for your business.
3.  Revise the chart of accounts for your business.
4.  Enter beginning balances from the October 1, 20XX balance sheet.
5.  Use QuickBooks:  Online Edition's help screens.
6.  Copy a QuickBooks:  Online Edition report into Microsoft Excel.
7.  Use one blank, formatted disk to back up report data.
8.  Complete activities for Part 2, New Company Setup.

**WEB OBJECTIVES:  In Part 2, you use the Internet to:**

1.  Access the Computer Accounting Essentials web site at www.mhhe.com/yachtessentials2e to check for updates.
2.  Log in to your QuickBooks:  Online Edition account.
3.  Enter your login name and password.
4.  Navigate the software.
5.  Complete Internet activities.

## COMPUTER ACCOUNTING ESSENTIALS WEBSITE

Before you begin your work in Part 2, New Company Setup, access the Computer Accounting Essentials web site at www.mhhe.com/yachtessentials2e. Select the QuickBooks link, and then link to Text Updates.  Check this web site regularly for reference and study.

### LOGGING IN TO QUICKBOOKS: ONLINE EDITION

Follow these steps to log in. You must have completed Part 1,
Downloading QuickBooks: Online Edition before starting Part 2, New
Company Setup.

1. If necessary, start your Internet browser.

2. There are two ways to go to QuickBooks: Online Edition's home
   page:

   a. Type http://oe.quickbooks.com in the "Address" box of your
      browser, then click on "Go."

   b. Click on the down arrow in the Address field. Select
      http://oe.quickbooks.com from the drop-down list.

3. Click on 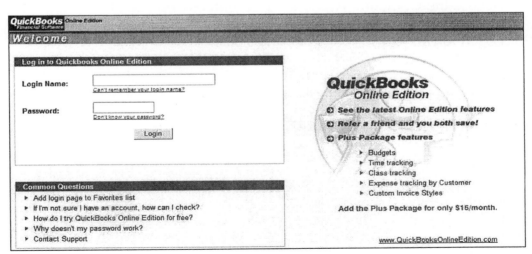 .

4. The "Welcome" screen appears.

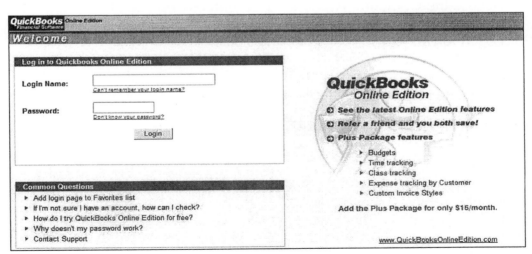

Complete the "Login Name" and "Password" fields. You *must* use the
same login name and password that you assigned on page 8 in the
QuickBooks Online interview, steps **3** and **4**.

Text and screen variations may occur since web-based software products backup and upgrade automatically.

5.  Click on [ Login ]. After a few moments your "Home" screen appears. Read the "Comment" box below, then continue with the next section, "Getting Started."

---

**Comment**
**When I log in, I get a "Security Warning" screen. What should I do?**

QuickBooks: Online Edition updates the software on a regular basis. Each time you log on you are using the current version of the software. If you try to log on and a screen similar to the one shown below appears, follow these steps.

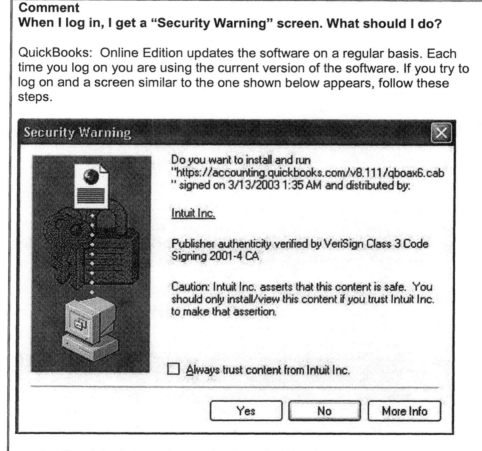

1.  Read the information on the Security Warning screen.
2.  Click [ Yes ].
3.  QuickBooks updated their software frequently. After clicking <Yes>, a screen may appear that includes the new features and enhancements added to QuickBooks: Online Edition.
4.  Read the information on the screen, then select [ Take Me to the Home Page ] (at the bottom of the screen). *Or,* if you want to print the screen, right-click, then left-click on "Print."
5.  Your company's home screen appears.

If a Security Warning pops up, you should check the Text Updates link on the book's website to see if there are recent changes to the book or software.

---

**READ ME**
**I can't remember my password. What should I do?**

1. Log in to QuickBooks: Online Edition (http://oe.quickbooks.com).
2. If necessary, enter your Login Name.
3. To reset your password, click on the link that says <u>Don't know your password?</u>
4. Answer the security question. Then, choose a new password and retype it. When
   through, click  OK .
5. Now go to your email inbox and retrieve the email that QuickBooks sent to you.
   Link to QuickBooks: Online Edition from the link within this email. The new
   password is activated.
6. Go to http://oe.quickbooks.com and log in with your new password.

## GETTING STARTED

1. When your home screen appears, move your mouse over the Company toolbar. When the pull down menu appears, click on "Preferences."

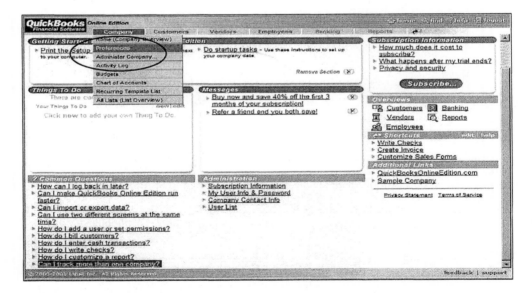

When the "Preferences" screen appears, complete the following steps:

- Company Contact Information: Verify that the Company name, address, email address, and phone number (if you typed a phone number) are correct.

- Company:
    i. Employee identification number (EIN). Leave this box blank.
    ii. First month of fiscal year: Use pull down arrow to select "October" as the first month of fiscal year.
    iii. First month of income tax year: Click on the radio button next to "January" as the first month of your income tax year. Compare your screen to the one shown below.

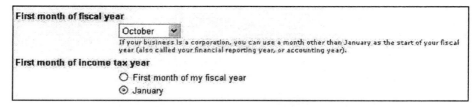

    iv. Tax form: Verify that the radio button next to "One or more shareholders" is selected.
    v. Closing the books: Leave this box blank.
    vi. Account numbers. This box should be unchecked.
    vii. Terminology for Customer: Verify that "Customers" is selected.
    viii. Email alerts. Leave this box blank.
    ix. Automatically apply credits. **Box must be unchecked.**
    x. Enable auto recall: Verify that the box is checked.
    xi. Read Restart setup interviews. Take no action.

- Categories
    i. Read income and expense accounts. Take no action.
    ii. Read Expense accounts. Take no action.
    iii. Standard products and services (for income accounts): This box should be checked.

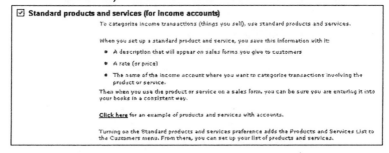

iv.  Location tracking. This box should be unchecked.
v.  Read Class tracking. Take no action.

- Sales Form Entry

    i.  Charges: This box **must be unchecked.**

---
☐ **Charges**

With QuickBooks Online Edition, you can always bill customers immediately by entering a charge directly on an invoice.

---

ii.  Read Custom fields. Take no action.
iii.  Custom transaction numbers. This box should be unchecked.
iv.  Deposits. This box should be unchecked.
v.  Discounts. This box should be unchecked.
vi.  Message to customers. Take no action.
vii.  Quantity and Rate. This box should be checked.

---
☑ **Quantity and Rate**

When selected, you can specify a quantity and rate for products and services as you enter sales. Entering quantity and rate lets you:

---

viii. Sales Tax. This box should be unchecked.
ix.  Service Dates. This box should be unchecked.
x.  Shipping. This box should be unchecked.
xi.  Terms. Verify that the "Default Invoice Terms" field shows "Net 30." If not, select it.

- Sales Form Delivery

    i.  Read Customize sales forms. Take no action.
    ii.  Delivery method default. Make sure that "Print" is selected.
    iii.  Read the Email message. Make no changes.
    **iv.**  Email sales forms as attachments. Read the information. **This box must be unchecked.**
    v.  Statements. Show aging information should be checked.
    vi.  Show summary or details. Select **show details**. Show details **must be** selected.

---

Text and screen variations may occur since web-based software products backup and upgrade automatically.

Show summary or details

Choose the amount of information to provide to your customers about each transaction.

○ **Show summary.**
Just one line appears for each invoice, sales receipt, or credit memo included on the statement. The only explanation your customer sees is the text you entered in the Memo field for the transaction.

In the example below, "Monthly maintenance" is text from the Memo field of invoice #7:

Invoice #7: Due 03/09/2002. Monthly maintenance.

◉ **Show details.**
An additional line appears for each charge or other line item in the transaction.

- Invoice Automation:
  i. Read Automation information.  Take no action.

- Accept Credit Cards: Read information: Take no Action.

- Vendors & Purchases
  i. Read the Expense tracking by customer information. Take no action.
  ii. Multiple split lines. This box should be unchecked.

☐ **Multiple split lines**

You "split" a transaction (such as a check or credit card charge) when you want to assign to it more than one account, typically expense accounts.

If you frequently enter split transactions, selecting this check box saves you the step of clicking Split between multiple accounts when you enter expenses.

    iii. Duplicate check warning. This box should be checked.
    iv. Duplicate bill warning. This box should be checked.

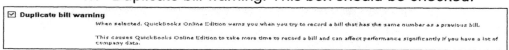

☑ **Duplicate bill warning**

When selected, QuickBooks Online Edition warns you when you try to record a bill that has the same number as a previous bill.

This causes QuickBooks Online Edition to take more time to record a bill and can affect performance significantly if you have a lot of company data.

    v. Terms. Read information. Take no action.

- Time tracking. Read information. Take no action.

- Reports:
  i. Default accounting method for summary reports. Verify that the radio button next to "Accrual" is selected.
  ii. Numbers format.  Verify that the radio button next to "Normally" is selected and that the box next to "Except zero amounts" is checked.

To complete the company interview, click on the  button at the bottom of your screen to save all of your preferences. In a few moments, your home screen will appear.

2. In the "Get Started with QuickBooks: Online Edition" area, click on <u>Start here </u>link.

3. Learn about QuickBooks Online Edition by taking interactive tours, experiment with a sample company, and get oriented by using the links located on your Welcome page.

4. When you are ready to proceed, click on [home] to return to your company's homepage.

5. As you know from your study of accounting, a *chart of* accounts is a list of all the accounts used by a company to conduct its business. The Chart of Accounts set up by QuickBooks: Online Edition for your company lists the names, types, and balances (if any) of accounts. To view the chart of accounts, move your mouse over "Company" on the QuickBooks: Online toolbar. Notice all accounts have "0.00" balances and no cash account is listed. Before deleting or editing the names of these accounts, you need to set up your cash account.

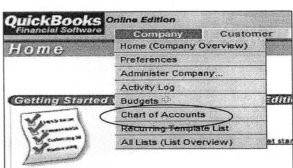

## SETTING UP THE CASH ACCOUNT

Follow these steps to set up your cash account.

1. To set up your Cash account, move your mouse over "Banking" on the QuickBooks: Online Edition toolbar. When the drop-down menu appears, click on "Banking Overview."

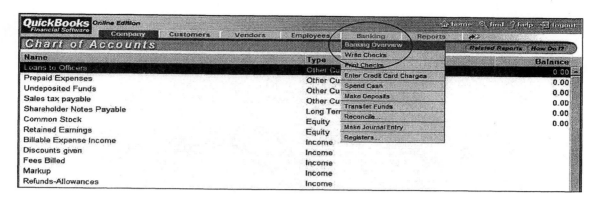

2.  In a few moments, the "Banking Overview" appears.  In the "Setup Tasks" list, move your mouse over "Set up a checking account" and click.

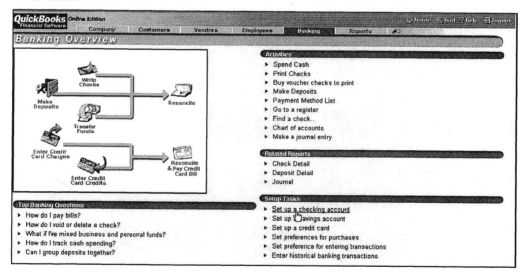

3.  A QuickBooks:  Online Edition - Mini Interview–Web Page Dialog box appears.  Type **XXXXXX** Service Corporation (X's indicate your first and last name).  Leave the subaccount box blank.  Type **Primary Checking Account** in the "Description" field.  Type **2000.00** in the "Balance" field. Type **10/01/20XX (use the current year, i.e., 2004 or 2005)** in the "as of" field.  Compare your screen to the one shown on the next page.

> **Comment**
> When using this text, fill in **all dates.**  If you do not fill in the date and year, QuickBooks will automatically assume your data is for today! *This is a common error when students make mistakes.*

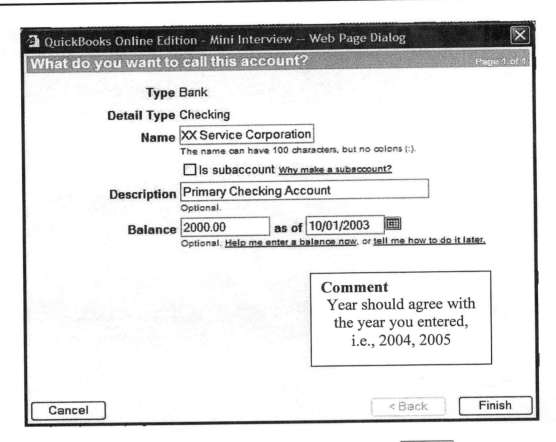

4. Review your entries, correct any errors, and click [ Finish ] when you are done.

---

**Comment:**
The business first started operations in a previous year. You are going to start recording transactions using QuickBooks: Online Edition as of October 1, 20XX (your current year ).

---

5. Return to your chart of accounts by accessing the chart of accounts from the Company drop-down list. Move your mouse over "Company" on the QuickBooks: Online Edition toolbar. When the drop-down menu appears, click on "Chart of Accounts."

---

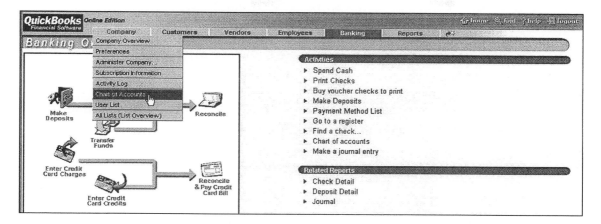

6.  Now your chart of accounts contains a bank type of account called "XXXXXXX Service Corporation" with a $2,000.00 balance. QuickBooks: Online Edition bank types of accounts are the cash accounts of the business. Notice the account requires a name more descriptive than just "cash."

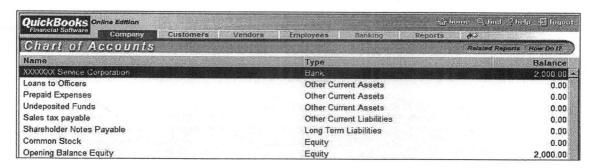

## REVISING THE CHART OF ACCOUNTS

Follow these steps to revise the chart of accounts.

1.  If necessary, access your chart of accounts by moving your mouse over "Company" on the QuickBooks: Online Edition toolbar. When the drop-down menu appears, click on "Chart of Accounts."

2.  When the QuickBooks: Online Edition constructed chart of accounts (based on your start up and preference interview answers) appears, you may want to scroll down this screen to see the entire chart of accounts. Since you will not be using all these accounts, let's revise some of these accounts.

### Deleting an Account

These instructions show you how to delete an account from the chart of accounts.

1. To delete an account you will not use, move your mouse over the account, clicking on it to select.

2. For example, to delete the account "Refunds-Allowances" highlight the account.

3. Click on **Delete**. (*Hint: The "Delete" button is at the bottom right of your screen.*)

4. A "Please Confirm—Web Page Dialog" pops up asking, "Are you sure you want to delete?"

5. Click on **Yes**.

6. In a few moments a revised chart of accounts will appear without the deleted account.

7. Delete the following accounts:

| | |
|---|---|
| Loans to Officers | Commissions & Fees |
| Shareholder Notes Payable | Other Income |
| Sales Tax Payable | Travel Meals |
| Discounts Given | Travel |
| Shipping Income | Taxes & Licenses |
| Promotional | Stationery & Printing |
| Miscellaneous | Business Income Tax-State/Local |
| Meals and Entertainment | Business Income Tax-Federal |
| Legal & Professional Fees | Compensation of Officers |
| Dues & Subscriptions | Penalties & Settlements |

There may be one or two additional accounts that QuickBooks: Online Edition will *not* allow you to delete. When you are finished with your chart of accounts, it will look similar to the one shown on the next page.

| Chart of Accounts | | Related Reports   How Do I? |
|---|---|---|
| **Name** | **Type** | **Balance** |
| XXXXXXX Service Corporation | Bank | 2,000.00 |
| Prepaid Expenses | Other Current Assets | 0.00 |
| Undeposited Funds | Other Current Assets | 0.00 |
| Common Stock | Equity | 0.00 |
| Opening Balance Equity | Equity | 2,000.00 |
| Retained Earnings | Equity | |
| Billable Expense Income | Income | |
| Fees Billed | Income | |
| Markup | Income | |
| Services | Income | |
| Advertising | Expenses | |
| Bank Charges | Expenses | |
| Insurance | Expenses | |
| Office Expenses | Expenses | |
| Rent or Lease | Expenses | |
| Repair & Maintenance | Expenses | |
| Supplies | Expenses | |
| Utilities | Expenses | |
| Other Income | Other Income | |

---

**Comment**

What if my Chart of Accounts list looks different?

Your chart of accounts may differ somewhat. Depending on which version of QuickBooks: Online Edition you are using, some accounts may not be deleted. These differences are insignificant. Along with the accounts you add in the next section, you will also learn how to add accounts "on the fly" later in the book.

---

**Adding an Account**

Follow these steps to add an account to the chart of accounts.

1. The chart of accounts list should be displayed on your screen. Click on the ⬬New⬬ button at the bottom of your screen.

2. A "QuickBooks: Online Edition-Mini Interview—Web Page Dialog" pops up asking what type of account would you like to set up. Since you will be setting up a fixed asset account, select the radio button next to "Choose from all account types." This is shown on the next page.

---

3. Click on [ Next > ] at the bottom of your screen.

4. Another "What type of account would you like to set up?" of the Mini Interview asks what type of account you would like to set up. Click on "Fixed assets" to select it and to see a description. Compare your screen to the one shown on the next page.

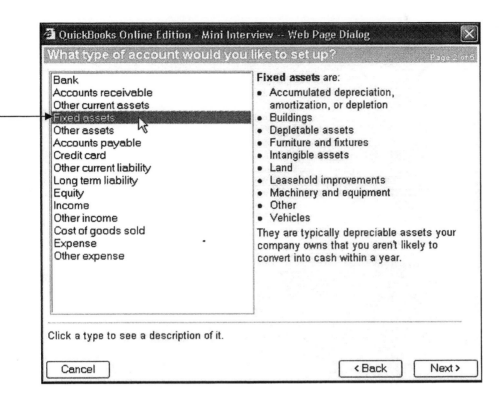

5. Click on [ Next > ] at the bottom of your screen.

6. "What type of fixed asset?" of the Mini Interview appears asking what type of fixed asset. Select "Machinery & Equipment" by clicking on it.

7. Click on [ Next > ] at the bottom of the screen.

8. "What do you want to call this account?" of the Mini Interview pops up asking several questions.

    a. Type **Computer Equipment** in the "Name" field.
    b. Leave the subaccount and Description boxes blank.
    c. To the question, "Do you want to track depreciation of this asset?" Select the "Yes" radio button.
    d. Review and revise your entries until you are satisfied.

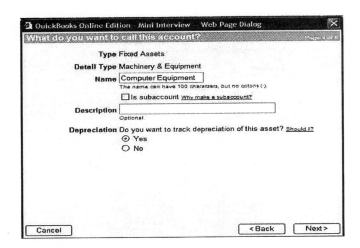

e.  Click on 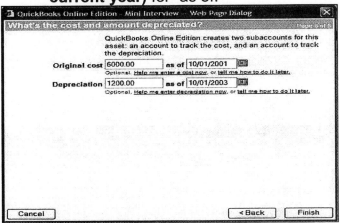.

9.  The Mini Interview concludes with "What's the cost and amount depreciated?"  Since the computer equipment was originally purchased for $6,000 on October 1, 2001, enter the following for the opening balances.

   a.  Type **6000** for "Original cost."  Type **10/01/2001** for "as of."
   b.  Type **1200** for "Depreciation."  Type **10/01/20XX (your current year)** for "as of."

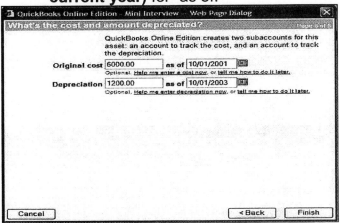

> **Comment**
> Year should agree with the year you entered, i.e., 2004, 2005

c.  Use the Back and Next buttons at the bottom of your screen to review and revise all your responses to the Mini interview. When you are satisfied, click on Finish at the bottom of your screen.

Text and screen variations may occur since web-based software products backup and upgrade automatically.

10.  Your chart of accounts will now contain the following accounts and balances for " Computer Equipment"

| Computer Equipment | Fixed Assets | 4,800.00 |
|---|---|---|
| Depreciation | Fixed Assets | -1,200.00 |
| Original Cost | Fixed Assets | 6,000.00 |

11.  Add an Accounts Receivable account.

    a.  From the chart of accounts screen, click on **New**.

    b.  What type of account: Select "Choose from all account types."

    c.  Type of account:  Select "Accounts Receivable."

    d.  Account name:  **Accounts Receivable** (leave Description blank).  When you are satisfied, click on Finish at the bottom of your screen.

**Changing an Account Name**

Follow these steps to make changes to the name of an account.

1.  The Chart of Accounts list should be displayed on your screen.

2.  Move your mouse over the "Supplies" account and click to select it.

3.  Click on the **Edit** button at the bottom of your screen.

4.  When the "Account Information" screen appears, place your cursor in the "Name" field and type **Computer** in front of "Supplies" so the "Name" field is changed to "Computer Supplies."

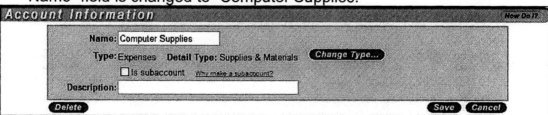

5.  Click on **Save**.

6. Your chart of accounts list will now show the account "Computer Supplies."

7. Use steps 2-6 to edit each of the following account names and descriptions:

| Name of Account | Change to | Description |
|---|---|---|
| Prepaid expenses | **Prepaid Insurance** | **Insurance paid in advance of use** |
| Depreciation (Fixed Assets) | **Accumulated Depreciation** | |
| Depreciation (Other Expense) | **Depreciation Expense** | |
| Opening balance-equity | **Paid in Capital** | **Opening balance** |

8. To check that your revisions were made, compare chart of accounts to the one shown below. (You may also have one or two additional accounts that QuickBooks: Online Edition will not allow you to delete.)

## Chart of Accounts

Related Reports  How Do I?

| Name | Type | Balance |
|---|---|---|
| XXXXXXX Service Corporation | Bank | 2,000.00 |
| Accounts Receivable | Accounts Receivable | 0.00 |
| Prepaid Insurance | Other Current Assets | 0.00 |
| Undeposited Funds | Other Current Assets | 0.00 |
| Computer Equipment | Fixed Assets | 4,800.00 |
| Accumulated Depreciation | Fixed Assets | -1,200.00 |
| Original Cost | Fixed Assets | 6,000.00 |
| Common Stock | Equity | 0.00 |
| Paid in Capital | Equity | 6,800.00 |
| Retained Earnings | Equity | |
| Billable Expense Income | Income | |
| Fees Billed | Income | |
| Markup | Income | |
| Services | Income | |
| Advertising | Expenses | |
| Bank Charges | Expenses | |
| Computer Supplies | Expenses | |
| Insurance | Expenses | |
| Office Expenses | Expenses | |
| Rent or Lease | Expenses | |
| Utilities | Expenses | |
| Interest Earned | Other Income | |
| Depreciation Expense | Other Expense | |

Text and screen variations may occur since web-based software products backup and upgrade automatically.

## BEGINNING BALANCE SHEET

On page 29 you recorded the opening balance for your business' checking account; and on page 36 you recorded the opening balance for your equipment and depreciation accounts.  Before you start recording transactions for your business, you need to record an additional beginning balance from the October 1, 2003 *balance sheet*.  As you know from your study of accounting, a balance sheet is a list of assets, liabilities, and stockholders' equity of a business as of a specific date.

The information in the Balance Sheet shown below will be the basis for recording opening account balances for your business.

| XXXXXXX [student's first and last name] Service Corporation Balance Sheet October 1, 20XX (Your current year) | | |
|---|---|---|
| ASSETS | | |
| Current Assets | | |
| Checking | $  2,000.00 | |
| Prepaid Insurance | 200.00 | |
| Total Current Assets | | $  2,200.00 |
| Fixed Assets | | |
| Computer Equipment | $  6,000.00 | |
| Accumulated Depreciation | (1,200.00) | |
| Total Fixed Assets | | 4,800.00 |
| **Total Assets** | | **$  7,000.00** |
| LIABILITIES & STOCKHOLDERS' EQUITY | | |
| Stockholders' Equity | | |
| Common Stock | $  1,000.00 | |
| Paid in Capital | 6,000.00 | |
| Retained Earnings | 0.00 | |
| **Total Liabilities & Equity** | | **$  7,000.00** |

Follow these steps to enter an opening account balance

1.  The chart of accounts list should be displayed on your screen.  All the opening account balances on the balance sheet have been entered *except for Prepaid Insurance and Common Stock*.  Let's enter the opening account balance for "Prepaid Insurance" now.

2. Move your mouse over the "Prepaid Insurance" account and click the account.

3. Click the ⬭Edit button on the bottom of your screen.

4. The Prepaid Insurance "Account Information" screen appears. Type **200** for the "Opening Balance." Type **10/01/20XX (your current year)** in the "as of" date field.

   (*Hint:* If you do not see "Opening Balance" and "as of" fields, you can enter an opening balance by using ▣help on the QuickBooks: Online Edition toolbar.)

5. Click on ⬭Save.

6. Now enter the opening balance for "Common Stock." Move your mouse over the "Common Stock" account and click the account. Click the ⬭Edit button on the bottom of your screen. The Common Stock "Account Information" screen appears. Type **1000** for the "Opening Balance" and type **10/01/20XX (your current year)** in the "as of" date field.

7. The chart of accounts now lists the "Prepaid Insurance" balance as $200 and the "Common Stock" balance as $1,000. Compare your chart of accounts with the one shown below. (This is a partial chart of accounts.)

| Chart of Accounts | | Related Reports How Do I? |
|---|---|---|
| **Name** | **Type** | **Balance** |
| XXXXXXX Service Corporation | Bank | 2,000.00 |
| Accounts Receivable | Accounts Receivable | 0.00 |
| Prepaid Insurance | Other Current Assets | 200.00 |
| Undeposited Funds | Other Current Assets | 0.00 |
| Computer Equipment | Fixed Assets | 4,800.00 |
|    Accumulated Depreciation | Fixed Assets | -1,200.00 |
|    Original Cost | Fixed Assets | 6,000.00 |
| Common Stock | Equity | 1,000.00 |
| Paid in Capital | Equity | 6,000.00 |
| Retained Earnings | Equity | |

The balances shown should agree with the October 1, 20XX (your current year) balance sheet shown on page 39.

## HELP SCREENS

Notice that every screen has a Help link on the QuickBooks: Online Edition toolbar.

1. Click on [?help] to see how the help screens work. Compare your screen to the one shown.

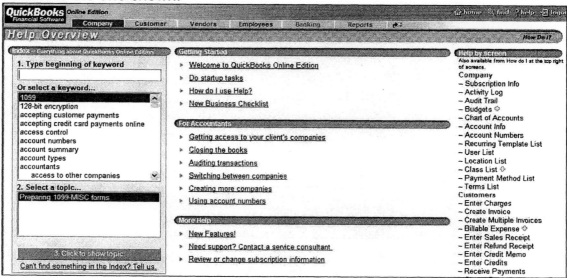

2. Read the information on the "Help Overview" screen to learn more. Notice that you can search by keyword or topic, seek help by screen, or get help by accessing various links; for example, Welcome to QuickBooks Online Edition, <u>Do startup tasks</u>, etc. These excellent built-in help features will help you whenever you have a question. DO NOT CONTACT A QUICKBOOKS SERVICE CONSULTANT.

## DISPLAYING THE BALANCE SHEET

To check that your balance sheet is correct, follow these steps.

1. Move your mouse over "Reports" on the QuickBooks: Online Edition toolbar. When the drop-down menu appears, click on "Balance Sheet." When the screen pops up that asks, "Which do you want as a default basis for accounting reports?" accept the default for "Accrual" by clicking on [ Finish ].

2. When the "Balance Sheet" appears it will be as of today's date. To change the date to October 1, 20XX (your current year), click on the **Customize...** button.

3. A "Customize Report: Balance Sheet—Web Page Dialog" pops up.

   a. For "Transaction Date" select "Custom" from the drop-down menu for dates. (*Hint: You may need to scroll up.*)
   b. Type **10/01/20XX (your current year)** in the "From" field.
   c. Type **10/01/20XX (your current year)** in the "To" field since this is the date of your company's opening balances.
   d. For "Accounting Method," make sure that "Accrual" is selected.
   e. For "Rows/Columns" if necessary, select "Total Only" from the drop-down menu.
   f. Review "Add Subcolumns for Comparison," "Lists," and "Numbers," but do not change.

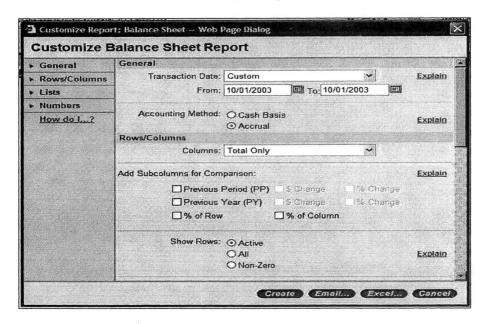

   g. Click the **Create** button.

4. The October 1, 20XX balance sheet for your business displays. Compare it to the one on page 39. Observe that at the bottom of your Balance Sheet screen, there are a number of links; for example, "See detail behind the numbers?," "What does "Split"

mean?." You may want to explore some of these links to learn more about your report.

To see how to save your balance sheet to Excel, continue with the next section, "Copying Report Data to Excel."

## COPYING REPORT DATA TO EXCEL

Copying and saving a report provides you with flexibility for reviewing and analyzing your business' data. You can easily copy QuickBooks:  Online Edition reports into a spreadsheet program like Excel and then save them to a disk.  You may want to use these features of QuickBooks:  Online Edition and Excel to back up your reports at periodic intervals.

To copy a report to Excel, follow these steps:

1.    The balance sheet should be displayed on your screen.

2.    In the upper left of your report screen, notice the Excel button. Click on the **Excel...** button to copy the report into Excel.

3.    The "File Download" screen appears. This screen confirms that you are downloading the file, and an Excel name is shown; for example, "report1.xls from accounting.quickbooks.com."  Click on Open .

4.    When the "Would you like to open the file or save it to your computer?" screen appears, click on Open .

5.    An Excel screen appears with your balance sheet.

6.    You may want to format your report and widen the columns in the report to fit the data.  To do so, move your mouse at the top of your spreadsheet to the line that divides two columns.  When your pointer changes to a cross-bar, double click. The columns should automatically widen to fit the data in them. Or, you can move the cross-bar to the right or left to widen or narrow the spreadsheet's columns.

| | A | B |
|---|---|---|
| 1 | **XXXXXXX Service Corporation** | |
| 2 | **Balance Sheet** | |
| 3 | As of October 1, 2003 | |
| 4 | | |
| 5 | | Total |
| 6 | ASSETS | |
| 7 | Current Assets | |
| 8 | Bank Accounts | |
| 9 | XXXXXXX Service Corporation | 2,000.00 |
| 10 | Total Bank Accounts | $        2,000.00 |
| 11 | Other Current Assets | |
| 12 | Prepaid Insurance | 200.00 |
| 13 | Total Other Current Assets | $         200.00 |
| 14 | Total Current Assets | $        2,200.00 |
| 15 | Fixed Assets | |
| 16 | Computer Equipment | |
| 17 | Accumulated Depreciation | -1,200.00 |
| 18 | Original Cost | 6,000.00 |
| 19 | Total Computer Equipment | $        4,800.00 |
| 20 | Total Fixed Assets | $        4,800.00 |
| 21 | TOTAL ASSETS | $        7,000.00 |
| 22 | LIABILITIES AND EQUITY | |
| 23 | Liabilities | |
| 24 | Total Liabilities | |
| 25 | Equity | |
| 26 | Common Stock | 1,000.00 |
| 27 | Paid in Capital | 6,000.00 |
| 28 | Retained Earnings | |
| 29 | Net Income | |
| 30 | Total Equity | $        7,000.00 |
| 31 | TOTAL LIABILITIES AND EQUITY | $        7,000.00 |
| 32 | | |
| 33 | | |
| 34 | | |

|◄  ◄  ►  ►|  \ **Balance Sheet** /

If you want to save your spreadsheet to a disk, complete the following steps.

1.  Put a blank, formatted disk in drive A.

2.  From the "File" menu choose Save As.

3. The "Save As" screen appears. Click on the down-arrow in the "Save in" box.  Select "3½ Floppy (A:)" to save to a floppy disk.  Or, if you prefer, save to your hard drive.

4. Type **opening balance sheet** in the "File name" box.

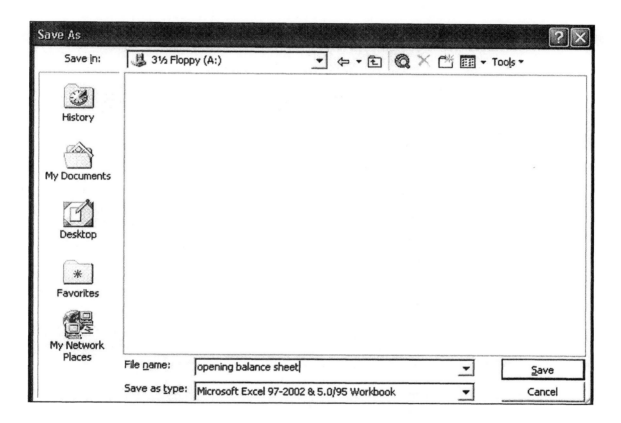

5. Click on the [    Save    ] button.  You can now open this file using Excel.

6. After saving this file, you are returned to the balance sheet screen in your spreadsheet program.  To close the spreadsheet program, click on the "X" button in the top right side of your screen.  You are returned to QuickBooks:  Online Edition's balance sheet.

To open this file in Excel, follow these steps:

1.  Go to your desktop and start Excel.

2.  From Excel's menu bar, click on File, Open. (Or, you can click on the   "Open folder" icon.)

3.  The "Open" screen appears. In the "Look in" box, select "3½ Floppy (A:)" for drive A (or if you saved this file to your hard drive, select that location).

4.  If necessary, select "All Microsoft Excel files" in the "Files of type" box.

5.  Click on the file named "opening balance sheet."

6.  Click on the [ Open ▾ ] button.  Your October 1, 20XX (your current year) balance sheet displays as an Excel spreadsheet.

7.  Exit Excel.

    Remember to use the Excel button feature of QuickBooks:  Online Edition to back up (save) your reports at periodic intervals.  For purposes of this exercise, the October 1, 20XX balance sheet was saved as "opening balance sheet." You could use a different filename; for example, "October 1 20XX balance sheet."

## LOGGING OUT OF QUICKBOOKS:  ONLINE EDITION

To log out of QuickBooks:  Online Edition, proceed with the following steps.

1. To log off, click on the [ logout ] button on the top right of your screen.

2. The "Welcome" screen appears.  You can log in again; or from the menu bar, click on "File" then "Close" to close your browser.

---

## CHECK YOUR PROGRESS

**Internet Homework:** To learn more about QuickBooks: Online Edition, follow these steps:

1. If necessary, start QuickBooks: Online Edition, and then log in to your account. (*Hint:* If you are already logged on, click ⌂ home).

2. When your "Home" screen appears, observe that the "Administration" area includes a link to Subscription Information. Link to it. Observe the date in the "Status" field.

   *Write the date of when your free trial ends:*

   11/24/05

3. Click 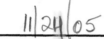. You are returned to your Home page.   In the "Common Questions" list, link to How can I log back in later?

4. Read the information on the screen, if you want--add a desktop icon link or to your favorites list, and then close the window.

**Multiple-Choice**.   In the space provided, write the letter that best answers each question.

_____1.   The two ways to log on to QuickBooks: Online Edition are:

   a.  Type http://oe.quickbooks.com in the "Address" box.
   b.  Click on the down arrow in the Address field and select the QuickBooks: Online Edition's web address.
   c.  Both a. and b.
   d.  There is only one way to log on.
   e.  None of the above.

_____2.   The first month for entering transactions is:

    a.  September.
    b.  October.
    c.  November.
    d.  December.
    e.  None of the above.

_____3.   The opening balance in the checking account is:

    a.  $2,000.00.
    b.  $10,000.00.
    c.  $25,000.00.
    d.  $8,000.00.
    e.  None of the above.

_____4.   The opening balance in the prepaid insurance account is:

    a.  $200.00.
    b.  $10,000.00.
    c.  $25,000.00.
    d.  $8,000.00.
    a.  None of the above.

_____5.   The default basis for accounting reports for your business is:

    a.  Cash.
    b.  Accrual.
    c.  Hybrid.
    d.  IRS.
    e.  None of the above.

_____6.   To change one of the accounts listed on the chart of accounts, you need to select which one of the following links?

    a.  Company Preferences.
    b.  Edit.
    c.  Number.
    d.  Account.
    e.  None of the above.

Text and screen variations may occur since web-based software products backup and upgrade automatically.

_____7.  The October 1, 20XX balance sheet for your business shows
         the following balance for Computer Equipment:

         a.  $6,000.00.
         b.  $8,000.00.
         c.  $4,800.00.
         d.  $7,500.00.
         e.  None of the above.

_____8.  The October 1, 20XX balance sheet for your business shows
         the following balance in your Paid in Capital account:

         a.  $7,000.00.
         b.  $10,000.00.
         c.  $6,000.00.
         d.  $2,000.00.
         e.  None of the above.

_____9.  To change the date on a QuickBooks:  Online Edition report,
         you should select which of the following icons?

         a.  Preferences tab.
         b.  Calendar.
         c.  Customize.
         d.  Login.
         e.  None of the above.

_____10. To obtain assistance about QuickBooks:  Online Edition, you
         should select which of the following links?

         a.  Startup.
         b.  Reporting.
         c.  Other.
         d.  Help.
         e.  None of the above.

**True/False.** Write T for True and F for false in the space provided.

_____11.   In Part 2 of *Computer Accounting Essentials Using QuickBooks: Online Edition*, you enter customers and vendors.

_____12.   The first month of the fiscal year for your business is December.

_____13.   You use the four links on the "Company" screen to set up a new company.

_____14.   There are five actions that can be taken from the chart of accounts screen: new, edit, delete, register, and report.

_____15.   A chart of accounts is a list of all the accounts used by a company.

_____16.   In QuickBooks: Online Edition, the company menu includes the chart of accounts.

_____17.   The balance sheet is a list of income and expenses on a specific date.

_____18.   In QuickBooks: Online Edition, the company menu includes the balance sheet.

_____19.   The balance sheet is reported as of today's date unless it is customized.

_____20.   To go back to the company preferences, you go to the company drop-down menu.

**Exercise 2-1.** Follow these steps to print a chart of accounts.

1.   Start your browser and login to QuickBooks: Online Edition in the usual way.

2.   When your home screen appears, select the "Reports" menu. Choose All Reports (Reports Overview).

3.   In the "Company" section, link to Account Listing.

4.  Click on the **Print...** button, and then make the selections to print in landscape orientation.

5.  *Optional:  From the "Account Listing" report screen, click on the* **Email...** *button. Email the report to your instructor. Type* **Your Name** *and* **Exercise 2-1** *as the Subject.*

6.  Continue with Exercise 2-2.

**Exercise 2-2**.  Follow these steps to print a balance sheet

1.  Click on the "Reports" menu.

2.  Link to the "Balance Sheet" on the drop-down menu.

3.  On the "Balance Sheet" screen, click on "Customize" to change the "Custom" dates from 10/01/20XX to 10/01/20XX (your current year).

4.  Generate the customized report, then make the selections to print in portrait orientation.

5.  *Optional: Click on the* **Email...** *button to email the report to your instructor. Type* **Your Name** *and* **Exercise 2-2** *as the Subject.*

6.  Click on **Logout** to exit QuickBooks:  Online Edition.

## PART 2 INDEX

# 3 Setting Accounting Defaults

In Part 3 of *Computer Accounting Essentials Using QuickBooks: Online Edition,* you will learn how to set **defaults**. Defaults are information or commands that the software or operating system automatically uses. QuickBooks: Online Edition refers to the setting of defaults as setting preferences. You can change default or preference settings by choosing another command. For example, QuickBooks: Online Edition has default margins and page lengths that you can reset.

**SOFTWARE OBJECTIVES: In Part 3, you use the software to:**

1. Set preferences for customer charges.
2. Set preferences for customer statements.
3. Set preferences for entering customer transactions.
4. Set up customers.
5. Set up products and services list.
6. Set preferences for entering vendor transactions.
7. Set up vendors.
8. Display the October 1, 20XX balance sheet.
9. Copy report data to Excel.
10. Complete activities for Part 3, Setting Accounting Preferences.

**WEB OBJECTIVES: In Part 3, you use the Internet to:**

1. Access the Computer Accounting Essentials website at www.mhhe.com/yachtessentials2e to check for updates.
2. Log in to your QuickBooks: Online Edition account.
3. Save the accounting preferences that you set with QuickBooks: Online Edition.
4. Complete Internet activities.

**COMPUTER ACCOUNTING ESSENTIALS WEBSITE**

Before you begin your work in Part 3, Setting Accounting Defaults, access the Computer Accounting Essentials web site at www.mhhe.com/yachtessentials2e. Select the QuickBooks link, and then link to Text Updates. Check this web site regularly for reference and study.

## GETTING STARTED

Follow these steps to start QuickBooks: Online Edition. You *must* complete Parts 1 and 2, pages 3 – 51 before starting Part 3, Setting Accounting Defaults. *The exercises at the end of each part must be completed, too.*

1.  Start your Internet browser and login to QuickBooks: Online Edition in the usual way.

---

**Comment:**
QuickBooks: Online Edition regularly updates their software. For this reason, you may see some differences between screen illustrations in the book and your screen display. Once you log on to QuickBooks: Online Edition, you will be using the latest software version. *Remember, websites are time and date sensitive and inevitably there will be some minor adjustments to the software.*

---

2.  Your "home page" screen displays. (*Hint: Your business name will differ from the one shown below. In Part 1 on page 9, the Company Information should include your name.*)

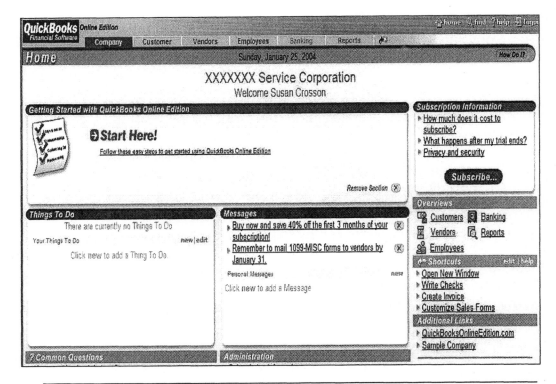

---

Text and screen variations may occur since web-based software products backup and upgrade automatically.

## CUSTOMER OVERVIEW

Before you can enter sales transactions, you need to set up information about customers. **Accounts receivable** are what customers owe a business. Credit transactions from customers are called **accounts receivable transactions**. In the next section, you will learn how to set up customer preferences and add credit customers for your business. Follow these steps to set up customer preferences for your business.

From the "Home" screen, move your mouse over Customers on the QuickBooks: Online Edition menu bar. When the drop-down menu appears, click on Customer Overview. The "Customer Overview" screen appears. In the next few steps you will be completing the tasks in the section called "Setup Tasks."

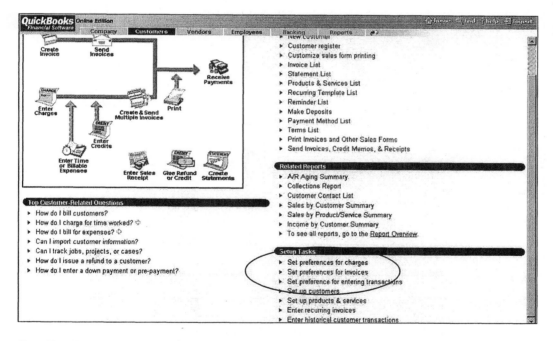

### Set Preferences for Customer Charges

1. In the Setup Tasks list, click on the link, Set preferences for charges. The "Mini Interview-Web Page Dialog screen appears. Continue with step 2 on the next page.

2. The "Charges Setup" dialog box asks about standard products and services. Read the information on this screen.

3. If necessary, click on the radio button next to "Yes," then click on [ Next > ]. This selection will carry over to how QB Online creates invoices. So make sure "Yes" is selected.

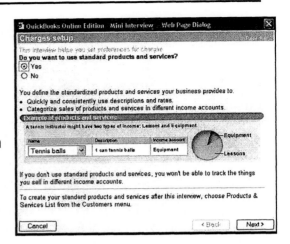

5. The "Tracking quantity and rate" dialog box appears.

6. Make sure the radio button next to "Yes" is selected, then click on [ Finish ]. You are returned to the "Customer Overview" screen.

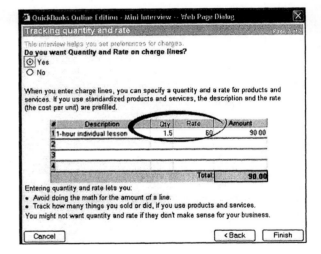

### Set Preferences for Customer Statements

1. From the "Customer Overview" screen, click on the link <u>Set preferences for invoices</u>. Continue with step 2 on the next page.

2. The "Due Date calculation" screen appears. Make sure that the "Default Invoice Terms" field shows Net 30.

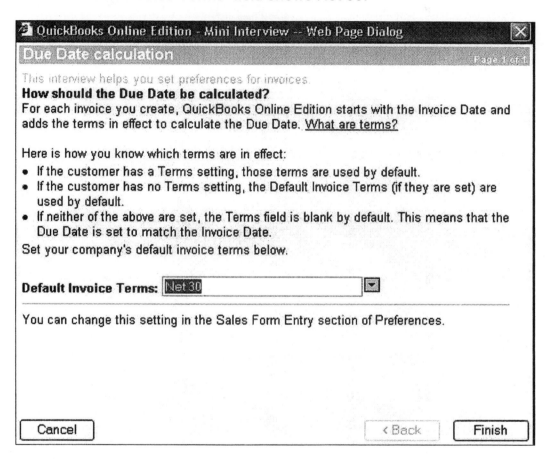

3. Click ⌈ Finish ⌋.

## Set Preferences for Entering Transactions

1. From the "Customer Overview" screen, click on the link <u>Set Preferences for entering transactions</u>. The "Do you want autorecall transactions?" dialog box appears. Accept the default for "Yes" by clicking on [ Finish ]. You are returned to the "Customer Overview" screen.

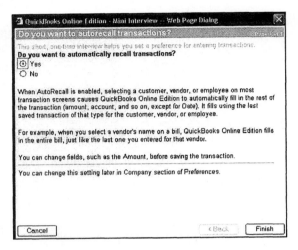

## Set up Customers:

To enter a customer record, complete the following steps.

1. From the "Customer Overview" screen, click on the link <u>Set up customers</u>. After a few moments a blank "Customer Information" screen appears. The "Customer Information" screen appears.

2. Complete the customer information for "Two Sisters B&B," a bed and breakfast business that provides their guests with wireless Internet services using the following screen as a guide. Use your tab key to move between data fields. The information that will record for Two Sisters B & B is shown on the next page.

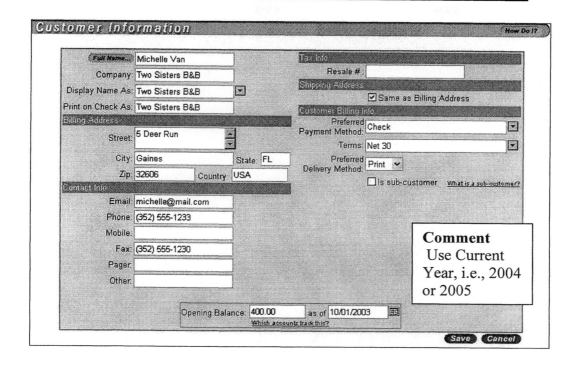

3. Check that you have entered the information correctly. *Hint: In the Display Name As field, select Two Sisters B&B.* Then click on **Save** to save the customer information for Two Sisters B&B.

4. Another blank "Customer Information" screen appears. Complete the customer information for "Connections Cafe," an Internet cafe business using the screen shown on the next page as a guide. Use your tab key to move between data fields. Check that you have entered the information correctly, (remember to select the company name in the Display Name As field), then click on **Save** to save the customer information for Connections Cafe.

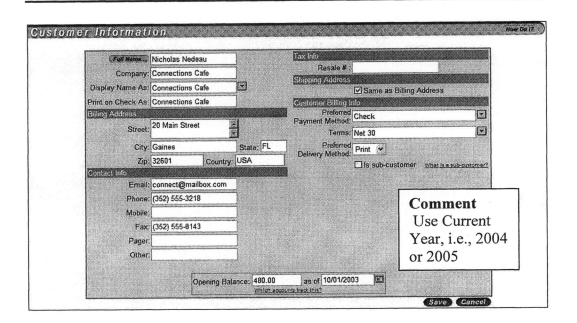

5. Another blank "Customer Information" screen appears. Complete the customer information for "Charity Access" a facility that provides Internet services for nonprofit organizations using the following screen as a guide. Use your tab key to move between data fields. Check that you have entered the information correctly, (remember to select the company name in the Display Name As field), then click on **Save** to save the customer information for Charity Access. The customer information is shown on the next page.

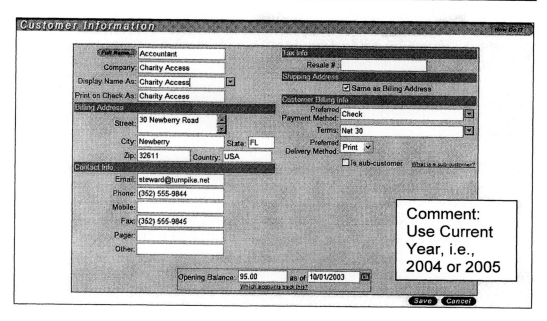

6.   Another blank "Customer Information" screen appears.  Move
     your mouse over "Customers" on the QuickBooks:  Online
     Edition menu bar.  When the drop-down menu appears, click on
     "Customer List."

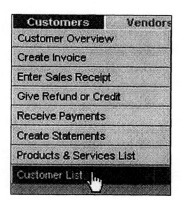

7. In a few moments the "Customer List" screen appears. Compare your customer list against the list of information about your three customer accounts below.

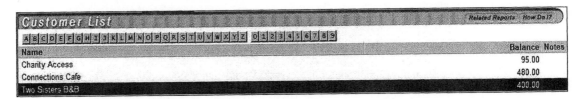

Observe that the balance for each customer is shown on this screen. When you check the balance sheet on page 68, you will see that the accounts receivable account has a balance of $975.

If necessary, you can edit the customer accounts by double clicking on the account, then selecting the *Edit* button.

8. Move your mouse over "Customers" on the QuickBooks: Online Edition menu bar. When the drop-down menu appears, click on "Customer Overview."

9. The "Customer Overview" screen appears. From the "Setup Tasks" list you have set preferences for customer charges, invoices, entering transactions, and set up customers. Next you will set up products and services.

## SET UP PRODUCTS & SERVICES

To set up your products and services proceed with the following steps.

1. From the "Customer Overview" screen, click on the link Set up products & services. After a few moments a blank "Product or Service Information" screen appears. Compare your screen with the one shown on the next page.

---

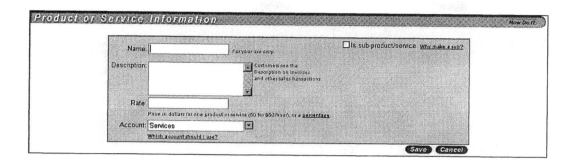

2.  Complete the product or service information for "Maintenance service" using the following screen as a guide.  Use your tab key to move between the "Name," "Description," "Rate," and "Account" fields. Check that you have entered the information correctly for maintenance service and then click **Save** to save the information on "Maintenance service."

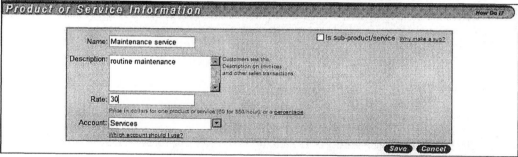

3.  Another blank "Product or Service Information" screen will appear.  For each of the items listed on the next page, complete a product or service information screen. Check to verify the information is correct and then click **Save**.  Each time a product or service is saved, a blank "Product or Service Information" screen will appear so that you can enter the next item.

| Name and Description | Rate per Hour | Account |
|---|---|---|
| New service | $100 | Services |
| Repair service | $ 50 | Services |
| Emergency service | $200 | Services |

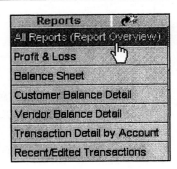

4. After completing and saving the "Product or Service Information" "Emergency service," another blank "Product or Information" screen will appear.  Move your mouse over "Reports" on the QuickBooks:  Online Edition menu bar, when the drop-down menu appears, click on All Reports (Report Overview).

5. Scroll down to the "Sales" list and link to Product/Service Price List.

6. Compare your "Products & Service Price List" to the one shown on the next page.  Correct any differences by clicking on the item needing correction to link to that item's Product or Service Information screen. Make the necessary corrections, then **Save**.  You are returned to the Product/Service Price List.

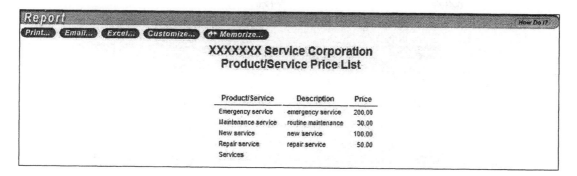

Observe that you can print, email, convert to Excel, customize or memorize this report.

9.   Click on [🏠 Home] to return to the "Home" screen.

## VENDOR OVERVIEW

Service businesses purchase the supplies they use from suppliers known as **vendors**.  Vendors are the businesses that offer your business credit to buy service and/or assets, or credit for expenses incurred.  When your business makes purchases on account from these vendors, the transactions are known as **accounts payable transactions.  Accounts Payable** is the amount of money the business owes to suppliers or vendors.

From your "Home" screen, move your mouse over "Vendors" on the QuickBooks:  Online Edition menu bar, when the drop-down menu appears click on Vendor Overview to see an overview of the vendor process.  In the next few steps you will be completing the tasks in the section called "Setup Tasks."

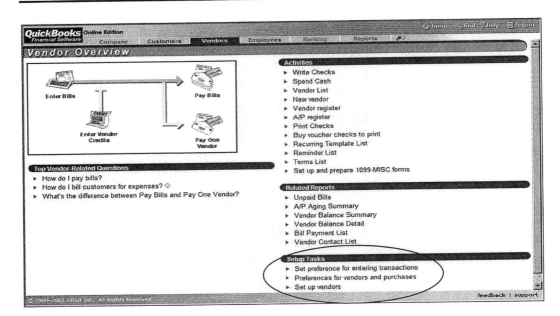

## Set Preferences for Entering Transactions

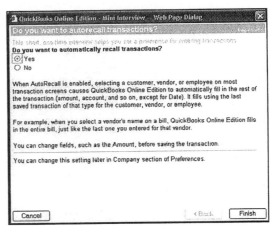

1.  From the "Vendor Overview" screen, click on the link Set preferences for entering transactions. After a few moments a "Mini Interview— Web Page Dialog" box appears asking do you want to automatically recall transactions. If necessary, click on the "Yes" radio button and then click on

    ⎿ Finish ⏌ at the bottom of the box to save vendor transaction preferences.

## Set up Vendors

Follow these steps to add vendors used by your business to purchase supplies.

1.  From the "Vendor Overview" screen, click on the link Set up vendors. After a few moments, a blank "Vendor Information" screen appears. Continue with step 2 to add a vendor.

Text and screen variations may occur since web-based software products backup and upgrade automatically.

2.  Complete the vendor information for "Big Bytes Supplies," a supplier that sells your business computer supplies using the screen below as a guide.  Remember, to select the company name (Big Bytes Supplies) in the "Display Name As" field. Use your tab key to move between data fields. Check that you have entered the information correctly, then click on **Save** to save the vendor information for Big Bytes Supplies.

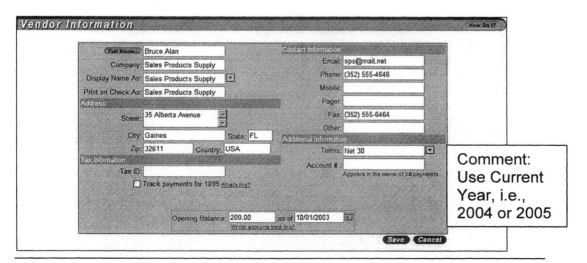

2.  Complete the vendor information for "Sales Products Supply," a supplier that sells your business office supplies using the screen below as a guide.  Use your tab key to move between data fields. Check that you have entered the information correctly, then click on **Save** to save the vendor information for Sales Products Supply.

2.   Another blank "Vendor Information" screen appears.  Move your mouse over "Vendors" on the QuickBooks:  Online Edition menu bar.  When the drop-down menu appears, click on "Vendor List."

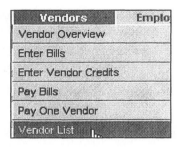

3.   After a few moments, the "Vendor List" appears.  Compare your "Vendor List" screen to the following screen.  Correct any differences by clicking on the vendor line needing correction to highlight it and then click **Edit** at the bottom of the screen.

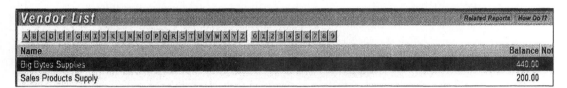

Observe that the balance for each vendor is shown on this screen. When you check the balance sheet below, you will see that the accounts payable account has a balance of $640.

4.   Move your mouse over "Vendors" on the QuickBooks:  Online Edition menu bar.  When the drop-down menu appears, click on "Vendor Overview."

5.   The "Vendor Overview" screen appears. From the "Setup Tasks" list, you have completed set preference for entering transactions and set up vendors.  Next you will display your balance sheet report.

**DISPLAYING THE BALANCE SHEET**

To display your balance sheet as of October 1, 20XX (your current year), follow the following steps.

1.   Click on "Reports" on the QuickBooks:  Online Edition menu bar, when the drop-down menu appears click on Balance Sheet.

---

Text and screen variations may occur since web-based software products backup and upgrade automatically.

2.    When the "Report" screen appears, click ▮Customize...▮. In the "Dates" filed, select "Custom."

3.    When the "Customize Report: Balance Sheet—Web Page Dialog" box appears, change the date "From" and "To" dates to 10/01/20XX.

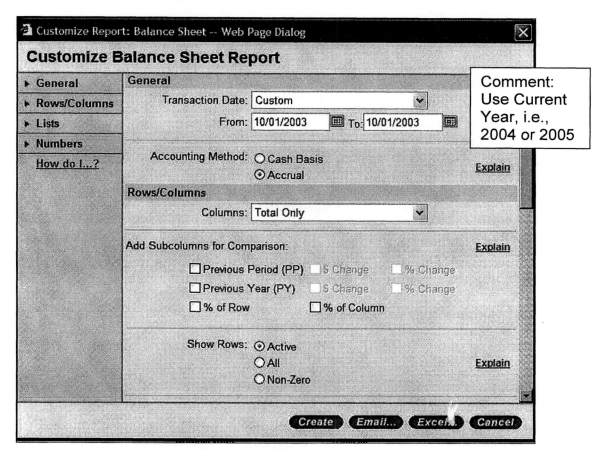

4.    Click on ▮Create▮. Your October 1, 20XX (your current year) balance sheet appears. Compare it to the one shown on the next page.

> **Note:**
> The Net income $335 which appears on the balance sheet is due to previous sales activity and resulted in the accounts receivable and accounts payable opening balances.

**XXXXXXX Service Corporation**
**Balance Sheet**
As of October 1, 2003

|  | Total |
|---|---|
| **ASSETS** | |
| Current Assets | |
| Bank Accounts | |
| XXXXXXX Service Corporation | 2,000.00 |
| Total Bank Accounts | $2,000.00 |
| Accounts Receivable | |
| Accounts Receivable | 975.00 |
| Total Accounts Receivable | $975.00 |
| Other Current Assets | |
| Prepaid Insurance | 200.00 |
| Total Other Current Assets | $200.00 |
| Total Current Assets | $3,175.00 |
| Fixed Assets | |
| Computer Equipment | |
| Accumulated Depreciation | -1,200.00 |
| Original Cost | 6,000.00 |
| Total Computer Equipment | $4,800.00 |
| Total Fixed Assets | $4,800.00 |
| **TOTAL ASSETS** | $7,975.00 |
| **LIABILITIES AND EQUITY** | |
| Liabilities | |
| Current Liabilities | |
| Accounts Payable | |
| Accounts Payable | 640.00 |
| Total Accounts Payable | $640.00 |
| Total Current Liabilities | $640.00 |
| Total Liabilities | $640.00 |
| Equity | |
| Common Stock | 1,000.00 |
| Paid In Capital | 6,000.00 |
| Retained Earnings | 0.00 |
| Net Income | 335.00 |
| Total Equity | $7,335.00 |
| **TOTAL LIABILITIES AND EQUITY** | $7,975.00 |

Text and screen variations may occur since web-based software products backup and upgrade automatically.

5. Verify that Accounts Receivable shows a balance of $975 and that Accounts Payable shows a balance of $640. Your company name should show "XXXXXX Service Corporation" (substitute the X's for your first and last name) and the date should show your current year.

6. Logoff or continue.

**CHECK YOUR PROGRESS**

**Internet Homework**

To learn more about the types of questions most frequently asked about managing customers and vendors in QuickBooks: Online Edition, follow these steps:

1. Click "Customers" on the QuickBooks: Online Edition menu bar. When the drop-down menu appears, click on "Customer Overview."

2. From the "Customer Overview" screen, click on at least two of the links under "Top Customer-Related Questions." For each of the selected links, write a short essay of what you learned. The minimum length of each essay should be 25 words; the maximum length 50 words.

3. From your "Home" screen, click "Vendors" on the QuickBooks: Online Edition menu bar. When the drop-down menu appears, click on Vendor Overview.

4. From the "Vendor Overview" screen, click on at least two of the links under "Top Vendor-Related Questions." For each of the selected links, write a short essay of what you learned. The minimum length of each essay should be 25 words; the maximum length 50 words.

5. Print one of the questions and answers and attach to your report. *(Hint: To print, select "Print" from the tool bar menu at the top of the "Help Topics—Web Page Dialog" box.)*

6. Use a word-processing program to type your reports. Start each essay with the question.

**Multiple-Choice**.  Write the letter that best answers each question.

_____1.  To enter customer records, you select:

    a.  Click on "New" on the "Customers List" screen.
    b.  Link to <u>Set up customers</u> on the "Customer Overview" screen.
    c.  Link to <u>New customer</u> on the "Customer Overview" screen.
    d.  All of the above.
    e.  None of the above.

_____2.  QuickBooks:  Online Edition information is saved via your
       Internet browser, when you click on:
    a.  Finish.
    b.  Help.
    c.  Setup.
    d.  Submit.
    e.  None of the above.

_____3.  The Products & Services List contains all of the following
       except:

    a.  Maintenance service.
    b.  Repair service.
    c.  Emergency service.
    d.  All of the above are included.
    e.  None of the above.

_____4.  All of the following are customers except:

    a.  Charity Access.
    b.  Big Bytes Supplies.
    c.  Connections Cafe.
    d.  Two Sisters B & B.
    e.  All of the above.

_____5.  All of the following are vendors except:

    a.  Big Bytes Supplies.
    b.  Sales Products Supply.
    c.  Connections Cafe.
    d.  All of the above.
    e.  None of the above.

_____6.  Service businesses purchase supplies from suppliers known as:

    a.  Customers.
    b.  Vendors.
    c.  Salespeople.
    d.  Clients.
    e.  None of the above.

_____7.  The amount of money a business owes to its vendors is called:

    a.  Accounts payable.
    b.  Accounts receivable.
    c.  Inventory accounts.
    d.  Service accounts.
    e.  None of the above.

_____8.  Account "Accounts Payable" is classified as a/an:

    a.  Expense account.
    b.  Liability account.
    c.  Equity account.
    d.  Cost of goods sold account.
    e.  None of the above.

_____9.  The amount of money credit customers owe to a business is called:

    a.  Accounts payable.
    b.  Accounts receivable.
    c.  Inventory account.
    d.  Service account.
    e.  None of the above.

_____10.   The October 1, 20XX balance sheet shows an accounts receivable balance of:

    a.   $975.00.
    b.   $200.00.
    c.   $640.00
    d.   $2,000.00
    e.   None of the above.

**True/False.** Write T for True and F for false in the space provided.

_____11.   Before you can enter credit sales transactions, you need to set up information about customers.

_____12.   Accounts receivable is what vendors owe to the business.

_____13.   Each time you click on the "Print" button, you are also saving.

_____14.   QuickBooks:  Online Edition refers to default settings as preferences.

_____15.   The opening balance for Connections Cafe is $480.00.

_____16.   When a service business makes purchases on account from vendors, the transactions are called accounts payable transactions.

_____17.   The types of service that service businesses sell to their customers are referred to as products and services.

_____18.   The opening balance for Two Sisters B & B is $400.00

_____19.   The opening balance for Big Bytes Supplies is $440.00.

_____20.   The opening balance for the Sales Products Supply is $400.00.

**Exercise 3-1:**  Follow these steps to print the customer list.

1.   If necessary, log in to your QuickBooks:  Online Edition account.

2.   From the "Home" screen, move your mouse over "Reports" on the QuickBooks:  Online Edition menu bar.  When the drop-down menu appears, click on "Customer Balance Detail.".

3.   Click on **Print...** to print the "Customer Balance Detail" report.

4.   *Optional: Email your report to your instructor.*

5.   Continue with Exercise 3-2.

**Exercise 3-2:**  Follow these steps to print the "Product/Service Price List."

1.   Click on "Reports, then select All Reports (Report Overview).  In the "Sales" section, link to Product/Service Price List.

2.   Click on **Print...** to print the Product/Service Price List report.

3.   *Optional: Email your report to your instructor.*

4.   Continue with Exercise 3-3.

**Exercise 3-3:**  Follow these steps to print the vendor list.

1.   Click on "Reports," then select "Vendor Balance Detail" from the QuickBooks:  Online Edition menu bar.

2.   Click on **Print...** to print the Vendor Balance Detail report.

3.   *Optional: Email your report to your instructor.*

4.   Continue with Exercise 3-4.

**Exercise 3-4:**  Follow these steps to print the balance sheet as of October 1, 20XX.

1. From the "Home" screen, move your mouse over "Reports" on the QuickBooks: Online Edition menu bar, when the drop-down menu appears click on "Balance Sheet."

2. When the "Report" screen appears, click on **Customize...**. Select "Custom" for the "Dates" field.

3. Type **10/01/20XX (Your current year)** in the "From" field, and **10/01/20XX (Your current year)** in the "To" field. Then click on **Create**.

4. Make the selections to print your report.

5. *Optional:  Email your report to your instructor.*

6. Back up your balance sheet using Excel.  (*Hint:  See the steps on pages 43 - 46, Copying Report Data to Excel.*)  Use **Your Name** and **Exercise 3-4** as the file name.

7. Print your spreadsheet balance sheet using Excel.

## PART 3 INDEX

# 4 Fourth Quarter Transactions

In Part 4 of *Computer Accounting Essentials Using QuickBooks: Online Edition*, you will record transactions for the fourth quarter of the year: October, November and December. You will record accounts payable, accounts receivable, and cash transactions. At the end of each month's transactions, you will also reconcile the bank statement.

## SOFTWARE OBJECTIVES: In Part 4, you use the software to:

1.  Record accounts payable transactions.
2.  Record accounts receivable transactions.
3.  Record cash transactions.
4.  Reconcile October, November, and December bank statements.
5.  Print reports.
6.  Copy report data to Excel.
7.  Complete activities for Part 4, Fourth Quarter Transactions.

## WEB OBJECTIVES: In Part 4, you use the Internet to:

1.  Access the Computer Accounting Essentials web site at www.mhhe.com/yachtessentials2e to check for updates.
2.  Log in to your QuickBooks: Online Edition account.
3.  Record fourth quarter transactions.
4.  Complete Internet activities.

## COMPUTER ACCOUNTING ESSENTIALS WEB SITE

Before you begin your work in Part 4, Fourth Quarter Transactions, access the Computer Accounting Essentials web site at www.mhhe.com/yachtessentials2e. Select the QuickBooks link, and then link to Text Updates. Check this web site regularly for reference and study.

## GETTING STARTED

Follow these steps to start QuickBooks:  Online Edition.  You *must* complete Parts 1, 2, and 3, pages 3 - 76, before starting Part 4, Fourth Quarter Transactions.  *The exercises at the end of each part must be completed, too.*

1.  Start your Internet browser and log in to QuickBooks:  Online Edition in the usual way.

2.  Move your mouse over "Vendors" on the QuickBooks:  Online Edition menu bar. When the drop-down menu appears, click on Enter Bills.  The "Enter Bills" screen appears.

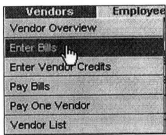

3.  Scroll down the "Enter Bills" page to the section on "How Do I..." Click on the various links to learn more about vendor-related transactions.

3.  For example, link to Edit a bill.  A "Help Topics--Web Page Dialog" box appears.  Compare your screen to the one shown on the right.

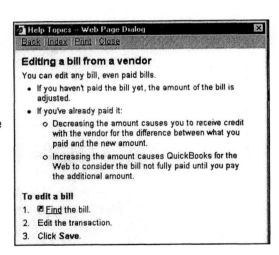

4.  After reading the information in the box, click ☒ in the upper right of the box to close the box and return to the "Enter Bills" screen.

5.  Repeat Steps 4 and 5 until all the links to the various "How Do I..." questions have been read.

6.  Return to the "Enter Bills" screen

## VENDOR TRANSACTIONS:  ENTER BILLS

Service businesses purchase the supplies they use from suppliers known as vendors.  Some of these vendors offer your business credit to buy supplies and/or assets, or credit for expenses incurred.  When your business makes purchases on account from these vendors, the transactions are known as accounts payable transactions.  Accounts payable, also known as the business' bills, is the amount of money the business owes to vendors or suppliers.

The "Enter Bills" screen is where you will enter information about the bills you receive from vendors. (Hint: Your screen illustration will differ somewhat—the "Bill Date" and "Due Date" fields will show the current date, *not* the dates shown below. Make no changes to the "Enter Bills" screen at this time.)

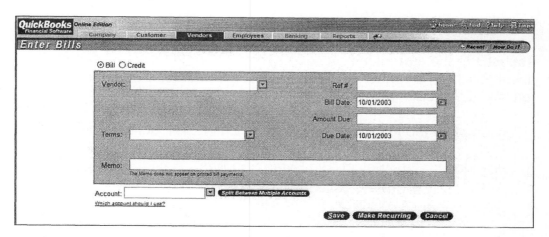

Your business purchases supplies on account from two vendors:  Big Bytes Supplies and Sales Products Supply.  You use the "Enter Bills" screen to record credit purchases.

Using QuickBooks:  Online Edition to track accounts payable is a two-step process:

1.  You use the "Enter Bills" window to record bills.  Entering bills as soon as you receive them keeps your cash flow reports up to date.

2.  You use the "Pay Bills" window to pay your bills to vendors. The "Pay Bills" window writes the checks for you.

## PURCHASES OF SUPPLIES:  ENTER BILLS

Follow these steps to enter bills from vendors.

1.  The "Enter Bills" screen should be shown on your screen.

2.   The transaction you are going to work with is

*Date*                *Transaction*

10/02/20XX[1]        Received Invoice 66JE and shipment from Big Bytes Supplies for the purchase of computer supplies that included the purchase of thumb drives on credit, Net 30, $300.

Here is how QuickBooks:  Online Edition journalizes this October 2, 20XX (substitute the current year for 20XX, i.e.2003 or 2004) purchase of inventory from a vendor.  Follow these steps to enter a purchase invoice on the "Enter Bills" screen.

1.   Complete the following fields on the "Enter Bills" screen:

Vendor          Select "Big Bytes Supplies"
Ref #           **66JE**
Date            Click on the "Calendar" icon.  Select "October 2, 20XX" as the date.  (In Part 2 on page 28, you set up the primary checking account as of 10/01/2003. If you used a different year, for example, 2004, be consistent.)
Amount          **300.00**
Terms           Observe that "Net 30" is shown in this field.
Due Date        Since this vendor is set up with terms of Net 30, 11/01/20XX" will appear in the "Due Date" field.

---

[1]In Part 2 on page 29, you set up the primary checking account to start as of 10/01/20XX (your current year). Make sure you use the same year consistently. In this text, 20XX's will be used to indicate the year.

---

Memo:                thumb drives
Account:            Select "Computer Supplies" (Note that this is an
                    Expense account)

2.  Compare your screen to the one shown below.

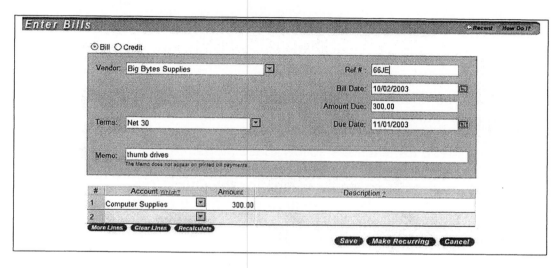

3.  When you are satisfied with your entry, click **Save** to post the
    information to your QuickBooks: Online Edition account.

4.  After a few moments, a new "Enter Bills" window appears and you are
    ready to record the next transaction. Record the following
    transactions using Steps 1-3 as your guide.

| Date | Transaction |
|---|---|
| 10/03/20XX | Received Invoice EX32 and shipment from Sales Products Supply for the purchase of office expenses that included the purchase of paper, printer cartridges, and message pads on credit, terms Net 30, $245. |

10/04/20XX        Received Invoice 89JE and shipment from Big Bytes
                  Supplies for the purchase of computer supplies that
                  included the purchase of memory cartridges and
                  memory sticks on credit, terms Net 30, $520.

10/05/20XX        Received Invoice EX45 and shipment from Sales
                  Products Supply for the credit purchase of office
                  expenses that included the purchase of office
                  supplies, Net 30, $385.

5.  When you have completed the each transaction, click on "Save."
    You are returned to the "Enter Bills" window.

To review these transactions, follow these steps.

1.  Move your mouse over "Company" on the QuickBooks: Online
    Edition menu bar.  When the drop-down menu appears, click on
    Chart of Accounts.  When the "Chart of Accounts" screen appears,
    double click on Accounts Payable.

2.  After a few moments, the "A/P Register" screen appears.
    This screen shows the total bills for your business, the four
    purchases made from vendors for $1,450 plus the opening balances
    in the two vendor accounts for a total Accounts payable of $2,090.00.
    This is the amount owed to vendors as of October 5, 20XX.

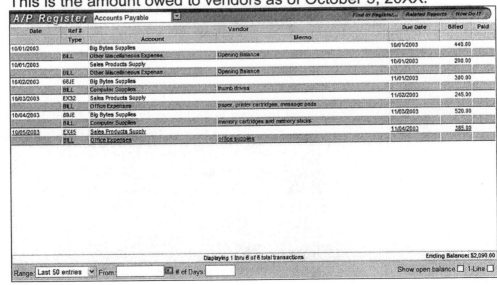

| Date | Ref # | | Vendor | | Due Date | Billed | Paid |
|------|-------|---|--------|---|----------|--------|------|
| | Type | Account | | Memo | | | |
| 10/01/2003 | | Big Bytes Supplies | | | 10/01/2003 | 440.00 | |
| | BILL | Other Miscellaneous Expense | Opening Balance | | | | |
| 10/01/2003 | | Sales Products Supply | | | 10/01/2003 | 200.00 | |
| | BILL | Other Miscellaneous Expense | Opening Balance | | | | |
| 10/02/2003 | 66JE | Big Bytes Supplies | | | 11/01/2003 | 300.00 | |
| | BILL | Computer Supplies | thumb drives | | | | |
| 10/03/2003 | EX32 | Sales Products Supply | | | 11/02/2003 | 245.00 | |
| | BILL | Office Expenses | paper, printer cartridges, message pads | | | | |
| 10/04/2003 | 89JE | Big Bytes Supplies | | | 11/03/2003 | 520.00 | |
| | BILL | Computer Supplies | memory cartridges and memory sticks | | | | |
| 10/05/2003 | EX45 | Sales Products Supply | | | 11/04/2003 | 385.00 | |
| | BILL | Office Expenses | office supplies | | | | |

Displaying 1 thru 6 of 6 total transactions          Ending Balance: $2,090.00

Range: Last 50 entries ▾   From:      # of Days:              Show open balance ☐  1-Line ☐

Text and screen variations may occur since web-based software products backup and upgrade automatically.

**Purchase Returns**:  **Enter Vendor Credits**

When supplies or an asset is returned to a vendor, the vendor issues a vendor credit to document the return.  In the next transaction, you are going to record a purchase return and revise your accounts to reflect the vendor credit.

Follow these steps to enter purchase returns.

1. Move your mouse over "Vendors" on the QuickBooks:  Online Edition menu bar. When the drop-down menu appears, click on <u>Enter Vendor Credits</u>.  The "Enter Vendor Credits" screen appears.

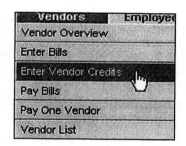

2. The transaction you are going to work with is:

   *Date*              *Transaction*

   10/05/20XX      Returned 1 thumb drive to Big Bytes Supplies, Invoice 66JE, $50.

Follow these steps to record the October 5, 20XX return of supplies.

1. The "Enter Vendor Credits" screen should be shown on your screen.

2. Complete the following fields:

   | | |
   |---|---|
   | Vendor | Select "Big Bytes Supplies" |
   | Reference No. | **66JE** |
   | Date | Select October 5, 20XX |
   | Credit Amount | **50.00** |
   | Memo | **Returned 1 thumb drive** |
   | Account | Computer Supplies |

   Compare your screen to the one shown on the next page.

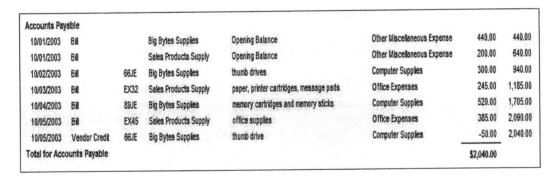

3. When you are satisfied with your entry, click **Save**.

4. To check that this vendor credit was entered in to your accounts, move your mouse over "Reports" on the QuickBooks: Online Edition menu bar. When the drop-down menu appears, click on <u>Transaction Detail by Account</u>. Customize the report so that "Display Options" are grouped by "Account;" Date Filters shows the "Dates" as "Custom" and "From" is shown as "10/01/20XX" and "To" is shown as "10/05/20XX." (*Hint:* Use the appropriate year.) When you locate the accounts payable information, observe that "Vendor Credit" reflects the $50 return of computer supplies on October 5, 20XX.

| Accounts Payable | | | | | | | |
|---|---|---|---|---|---|---|---|
| 10/01/2003 | Bill | | Big Bytes Supplies | Opening Balance | Other Miscellaneous Expense | 440.00 | 440.00 |
| 10/01/2003 | Bill | | Sales Products Supply | Opening Balance | Other Miscellaneous Expense | 200.00 | 640.00 |
| 10/02/2003 | Bill | 66JE | Big Bytes Supplies | thumb drives | Computer Supplies | 300.00 | 940.00 |
| 10/03/2003 | Bill | EX32 | Sales Products Supply | paper, printer cartridges, message pads | Office Expenses | 245.00 | 1,185.00 |
| 10/04/2003 | Bill | 89JE | Big Bytes Supplies | memory cartridges and memory sticks | Computer Supplies | 520.00 | 1,705.00 |
| 10/05/2003 | Bill | EX45 | Sales Products Supply | office supplies | Office Expenses | 385.00 | 2,090.00 |
| 10/05/2003 | Vendor Credit | 66JE | Big Bytes Supplies | thumb drive | Computer Supplies | -50.00 | 2,040.00 |
| Total for Accounts Payable | | | | | | | $2,040.00 |

5. Move your mouse over "Vendors" on the QuickBooks: Online Edition menu bar. When the drop-down menu appears, click on <u>Vendor Overview</u>. The "Vendor Overview" screen appears.

**Vendor Payments:  Pay Bills**

You have recorded four bills to vendors and one return.  The credit terms offered to your business by each vendor is Net 30.

You are going to record the following vendor payment:

*Date*                    *Transaction*

10/06/20XX      Paid Big Bytes Supplies' $440 opening balance by hand-writing a check (# 1) for $390 and applying the October 5 vendor credit for $50.  (*Hint:  Your business' opening balance was $440.  On October 5, you returned one thumb drive for a $50 credit.  The balance owed to Big Bytes Supplies after the return is $390, excluding any purchases made during October.*)

Follow these steps to record vendor payments.

1.  Move your mouse over "Vendors" on the QuickBooks:  Online Edition menu bar.  When the drop-down menu appears, click on Pay Bills. The "Pay Bills" window appears.

2.  Click on the radio button to show all bills.

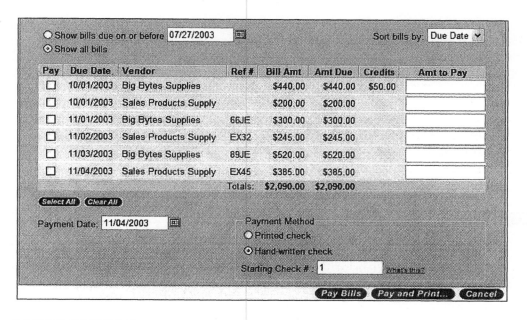

3. Complete the following:

| | |
|---|---|
| Pay | Place a check mark in the box next to the first vendor "Big Bytes Supplies" on the list. |
| Amount to Pay | $390 (Observe that this amount is completed automatically.) |
| Payment Date | **10/06/20XX** |
| Payment Method | Select Hand-written check |
| Starting Check # | 1 |

4. Compare your screen to the one shown below.

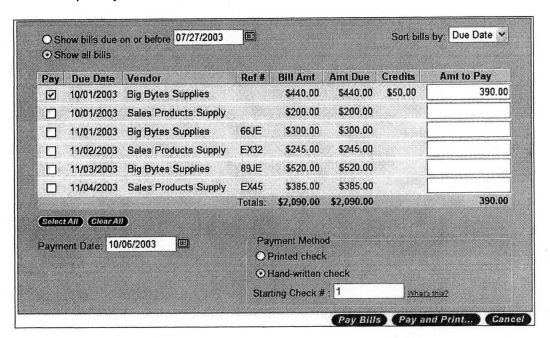

5. When you are satisfied with your work, click **Pay Bills**. The following screen shows that 1 bill is paid. Go to the "Bill Payment List" screen by clicking on it. (*Hint:* The "Created" line will show the current date.)

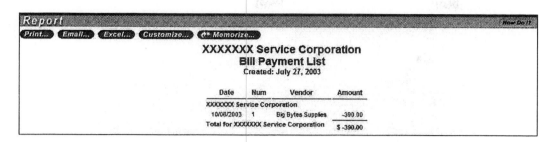

6. Using Steps 1-4 as a guide, pay the following bills with hand-written checks. (*Hint*: Remember to select "Show all bills.")

Date                    Transactions

10/07/20XX              Paid Sales Products Supply, Invoice EX32, $245 for the October 3 purchase with check number 2.

10/07/20XX              Paid Big Bytes Supplies, Invoice 66JE, $300 for the October 4 purchase with check number 3.

7. Compare your "Bill Payment List" report to the one shown below.

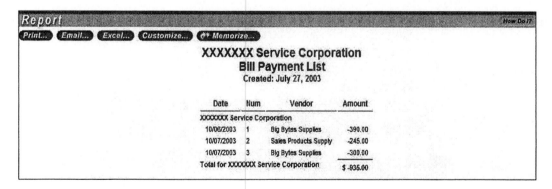

8. To check that the vendor payments were made, display the "Transaction List by Vendor." (*Hint:* Move your mouse over "Reports" on the QuickBooks: Online Edition menu bar. When the drop-down menu appears, click on All Reports (Report Overview). When the "Reports Overview" screen appears, click on the link to Transaction List by Vendor. Remember to customize the report changing the "From:" date to 10/01/20XX and the "To" date to 10/10/20XX. Click on the Create button to display the report.)

```
Report                                                                    How Do I?
Print...  Email...  Excel...  Customize...  ↻ Memorize...

                        XXXXXXX Service Corporation
                        Transaction List by Vendor
                              October 1-10, 2003

         Date         Type          Num    Memo/Description              Account              Amount
    Big Bytes Supplies
         10/01/2003   Bill                 Opening Balance               Accounts Payable        440.00
         10/02/2003   Bill          66JE   thumb drives                  Accounts Payable        300.00
         10/04/2003   Bill          89JE   memory cartridges and memory sticks  Accounts Payable 520.00
         10/05/2003   Vendor Credit 66JE   thumb drive                   Accounts Payable        -50.00
         10/06/2003   Bill Payment (Check)  1                            XXXXXXX Service Corporation  -390.00
         10/07/2003   Bill Payment (Check)  3                            XXXXXXX Service Corporation  -300.00

    Sales Products Supply
         10/01/2003   Bill                 Opening Balance               Accounts Payable        200.00
         10/03/2003   Bill          EX32   paper, printer cartridges, message pads  Accounts Payable  245.00
         10/05/2003   Bill          EX45   office supplies               Accounts Payable        385.00
         10/07/2003   Bill Payment (Check)  2                            XXXXXXX Service Corporation  -245.00
```

9.  Compare your "Transaction List by Vendor" to the one shown above. (In the "Account" column your company name will show instead of "XXXXXXX Service Corporation.")

10.  You may want to log off or continue with the next section.

## CUSTOMER TRANSACTIONS:  CREATE INVOICE

When you sell services to credit customers, the amount of those sales are recorded in an account called accounts receivable.  In the following section, you will record credit customer transactions.

In QuickBooks:  Online Edition, the second selection in the "Customers" drop-down menu is "Create Invoice."  You use the Create Invoice link to record credit customer transactions.

Before you start, let's review your business' credit customers.

- Two Sisters B&B:  Your business has offered credit terms of "Net 30" meaning the full amount is due within 30 days of the invoice date.
- Connections Cafe:  This customer also has credit terms of "Net 30" extended to them.
- Charity Access:  This facility also has credit terms of "Net 30."

Text and screen variations may occur since web-based software products backup and upgrade automatically.

The transaction you are going to work with is:

*Date*              *Transaction*

10/08/20XX      Sold services on account to Two Sisters B&B, Invoice
                No. 1004 for $1,200 which included 12 hours new
                service at $100 per hour due to the installation of a
                wireless network.

---

**Comment**
QuickBooks automatically numbers invoices, unless you change the default to custom.
On the next page, you accept the default for "Automatic." The invoice number for the
10/8/20XX transaction is 1004. Invoice numbers 1001, 1002 and 1003 were applied to
the opening balances.

---

Follow these steps to record credit sales.

1. From the menu bar, click on Customers, then Create Invoice. The
   "Create Invoice" screen appears.

2. A "Mini-Interview—Web Page Dialog" screen pops up. Make sure
   that "No" is selected in answer to the question "Do you enter charges
   and bill for them later?"

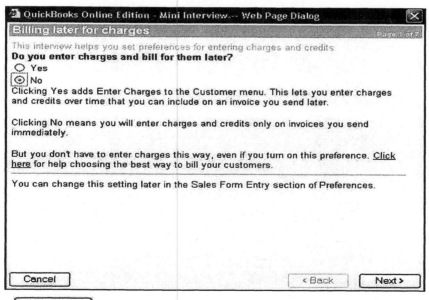

3. Click [ Next > ] .

---

4. The "Custom transaction numbers" screen appears. next

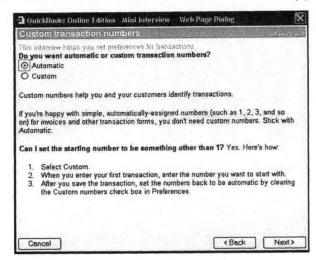

5. Click 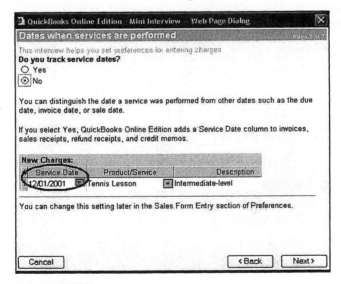 .

6. The "Dates when services are performed" screen appears.

7. Click .

---

8. The "Discounts, shipping, and deposits" screen appears.

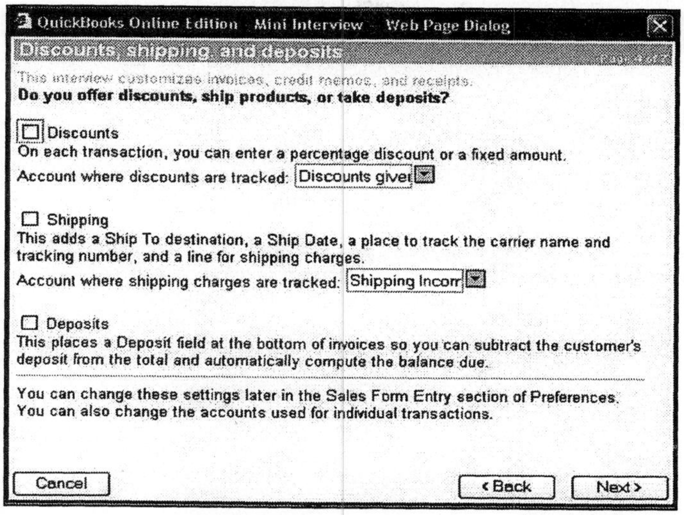


9. Make sure each box is unchecked. Click Next >.

10. The "Sales Tax" screen appears. Make sure "No" is selected.

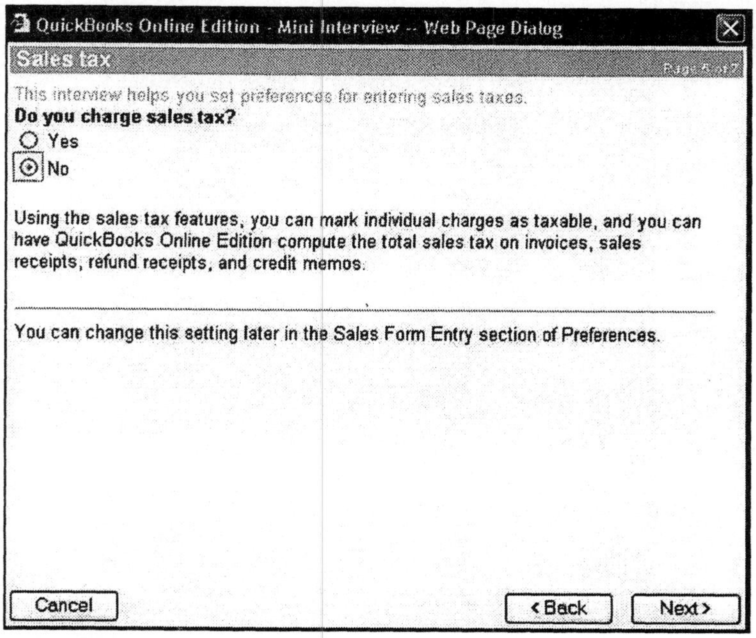


11. Click Next >.

12.  The "Custom fields on transactions" screen appears.

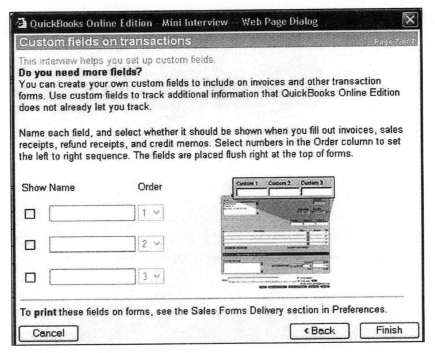

13.  Read the information on this screen. Take no action. Then click
     Finish . The "Create Invoice" screen appears. Compare it to the
     one shown on the next page.

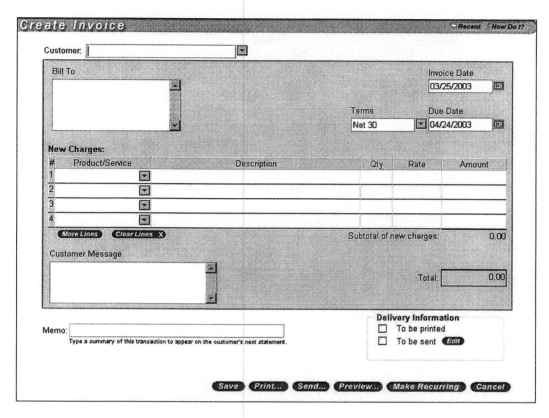

14. Complete the following fields:

| | |
|---|---|
| Customer | Select "Two Sisters B&B" |
| Date: | **10/8/20XX** (Use the current year) |
| Product/Service 1 | Select "New service" |
| Quantity | **12** |
| Rate | 100 is completed automatically |
| Amount | 1,200.00 is completed automatically. |
| | |
| Memo | Install wireless network. |

15. Compare your "Create Invoice" screen to the one shown on the next page.

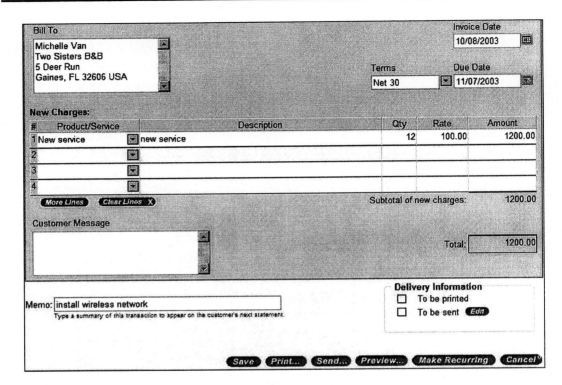

16. Make sure "To be printed" is unchecked. When you are satisfied with your work, click **Save** to post the information to your QuickBooks: Online Edition account.

17. After a few moments, a new "Create Invoice" window appears and you are ready to record the next transaction. Record the following accounts receivable transactions using Steps 1-3 as your guide.

| Date | Transactions |
|------|-------------|
| 10/09/20XX | Sold maintenance services on account to Charity Access, Invoice No. 1005, for a total of $300 for 10 hours of maintenance work at $30 per hour. (Hint: Remember, "To be printed" should be unchecked.) |

10/10/20XX    Sold services on account to Connections Cafe, Invoice No. 1006, $780 for 6 hours of maintenance services at $30 per hour and 12 hours of repair services at $50 per hour.

10/11/20XX    Sold services on account to Two Sisters B&B, Invoice 1007, $540 for 8 hours of maintenance services at $30 per hour and 1.5 hours of emergency services at $200 per hour.

### Sales Returns and Allowances:  Give Credit or Refund

The "Customers" drop-down menu on the QuickBooks:  Online Edition menu bar includes a link to "Give Refund or Credit."  When credit customers are dissatisfied, you use the Give Refund or Credit link.

The sales credit transaction you are going to work with is:

*Date*          *Transaction*

10/13/20XX    Two Sisters B&B received a $150 reduction in their October 8 Invoice (#1004) due to damage done to a wall during the wireless network installation. (This is numbered Credit Memo 1008.)

1. Move your mouse over "Customers" on the QuickBooks:  Online Edition menu bar.  When the drop-down menu appears, click on "Enter Refund or Credit."

2. The "Give a Credit or Refund to a Customer" screen appears. Select "Credit."

3. Make sure that "Give credit for something already billed

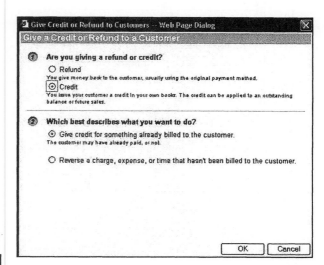

to the customer is selected." Then click [ OK ]. If the "Web Page Dialog screen on "Automatically Apply Credits" appears, confirm that this preference is not selected and click [ OK ]. The "Enter Credit Memo" screen appears.

4. Complete the following fields:

| | |
|---|---|
| Customer | Select "Two Sisters B&B" |
| Date | 10/13/20XX |
| Product/Service 1 | New installation |
| Quantity | **1.5** |
| Rate | 100 |
| Amount | 150.00 |
| | |
| Memo | Credit due to wall damage. Uncheck "To be printed." |

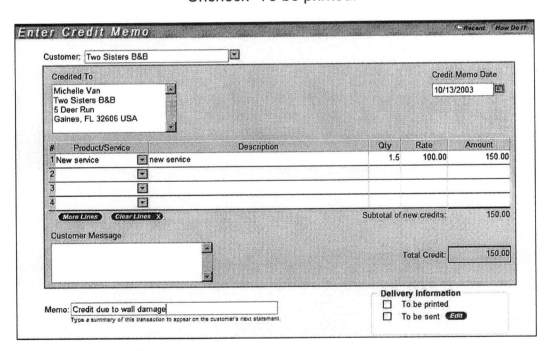

5. Click [ Save ].

**Displaying the Accounts Receivable Register**

To see that your customer transactions and credit memo have been recorded, display the "Transaction List by Customer."

1.  Move your mouse over "Reports" on the QuickBooks: Online Edition menu bar. When the drop-down menu appears, click on All Reports (Report Overview).

2.  When the "Reports Overview" screen appears, click on the link to <u>Transaction List by Customer</u>.

3.  Click **Customize...** button on the "Transaction List by Customer" screen. When the "Customize Report—Web Page Dialog" box pops up, select "Custom" for the Date Options. For the "From:" date enter 10/01/20XX and for the "To:" date enter 10/15/20XX. Click <Createt> at the bottom of the screen to display the report.

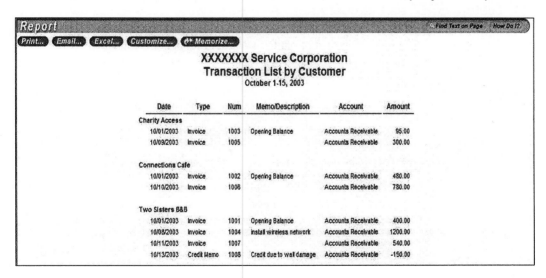

| Date | Type | Num | Memo/Description | Account | Amount |
|---|---|---|---|---|---|
| **Charity Access** | | | | | |
| 10/01/2003 | Invoice | 1003 | Opening Balance | Accounts Receivable | 95.00 |
| 10/09/2003 | Invoice | 1005 | | Accounts Receivable | 300.00 |
| **Connections Cafe** | | | | | |
| 10/01/2003 | Invoice | 1002 | Opening Balance | Accounts Receivable | 480.00 |
| 10/10/2003 | Invoice | 1006 | | Accounts Receivable | 780.00 |
| **Two Sisters B&B** | | | | | |
| 10/01/2003 | Invoice | 1001 | Opening Balance | Accounts Receivable | 400.00 |
| 10/08/2003 | Invoice | 1004 | install wireless network | Accounts Receivable | 1200.00 |
| 10/11/2003 | Invoice | 1007 | | Accounts Receivable | 540.00 |
| 10/13/2003 | Credit Memo | 1008 | Credit due to wall damage | Accounts Receivable | -150.00 |

**Comment**

Your "Num" column may differ. You can ignore these differences; they are usually insignificant. Remember QB Online Edition assigns numbers automatically.

If you move your mouse over the date of any of the transactions, you can link to that record and edit the entry, if necessary.

### Receipts From Customers:  Receive Customer Payments

Once you issue an invoice to a customer that customer owes your business money.  It is easy to apply customer payments in QuickBooks:  Online Edition.  From the "Customer" drop-down menu you select the link to "Receive Payments."

In Part 3, you entered an opening balance for Two Sisters B&B of $400.  The transaction that follows shows you how to record payment from Two Sisters B&B of that opening balance and apply the $150 credit memo to their account.

1.  Move your mouse over "Customers" on the QuickBooks:  Online Edition menu bar.  When the drop-down menu appears, click on the link to Receive Payments.  The "Receive Payments" screen appears.

2.  Select the date "10/13/20XX" from the calendar icon and select "Two Sisters B&B" as the customer.  A "Please wait.  Retrieving customer information" box appears.  In a few moments, the "Receive Payments" screen reappears with Two Sisters B&B credits and outstanding statement charges.

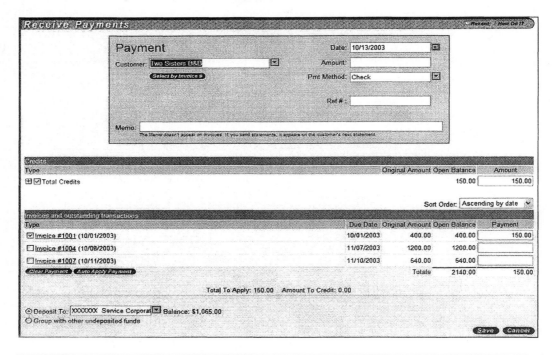

Text and screen variations may occur since web-based software products backup and upgrade automatically.

3. Complete the following fields:

| | |
|---|---|
| Deposit To | "XXXXXXX Service Corporation" is automatically completed. |
| Amount | Type **400.00** |
| Pmt Method: | "Check" is automatically completed. |
| Ref # | Type **9290** |
| Memo | Opening balance |

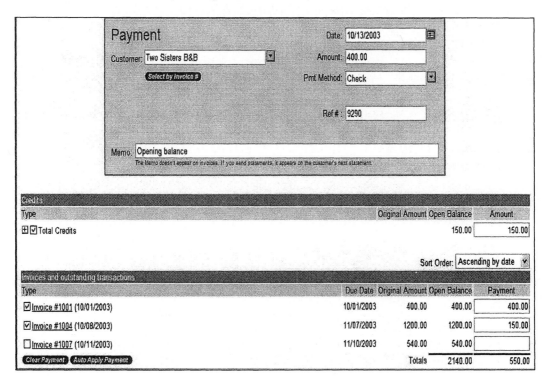

4. Click **Save**. A new "Receive Payments" screen appears.

5.  Complete the following transactions:

*Date*            *Transactions*

10/16/20XX     Received a check from Connections Cafe in payment of their opening balance, $480.00, Check No. 4522.

10/16/20XX     Received a check from Charity Access in payment of their opening balance, $95.00, Check No. 816.

10/16/20XX     Received a $1,050 check from Two Sisters B&B in payment of October 7 invoice, less the October 13 credit memo, Check No. 9346.

10/18/20XX     Received a $300 check from Charity Access in payment of October 9 Invoice, Check No. 901.

10/19/20XX     Received a $780 check from Connections Cafe in payment of October 10 Invoice, Check No. 5001.

10/19/20XX     Received a $540 check from Two Sisters B&B in payment of October 11 Invoice, Check No. 9401.

To verify that these payments were recorded in accounts receivable, follow these steps to display the "Accounts Receivable Register":

1.  Move your mouse over "Company" on the QuickBooks: Online Edition menu bar. When the drop-down menu appears, click on Chart of Accounts.

2.  When the "Chart of Accounts" screen appears, double click on Accounts Receivable to view the "A/R Register."

> **Hint:**
> To have a one-line view of the A/R Register, click in the "1-Line" box in the lower right of the A/R Register screen.

3.  Scroll down the "A/R Register" screen. The "Balance" shows "$0.00." Compare your screen to the one shown on the next page.

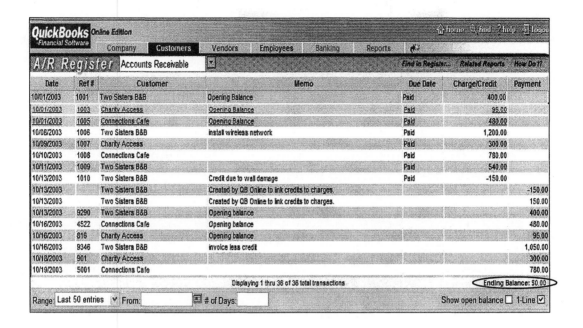

## CASH TRANSACTIONS

Your business makes cash sales and cash payments.  The transactions that follow will show you how to use the Enter "Sales Receipts" link under "Customers" and use the "Write Checks" link under "Banking" on the QuickBooks:  Online Edition menu bar.

### Cash Sales:  Enter Sales Receipts

The transaction for a cash sale follows.

| Date | Transaction |
|------|-------------|
| 10/20/20XX | Cash sales of various repairs, $2,150, received check No. 801. |

1.  Move your mouse over "Customers" on the QuickBooks:  Online Edition menu bar.  When the drop-down menu appears, click on Enter Sales Receipts.  The "Enter Sales Receipts" window appears.

2. In the "Customer" field, type **Cash Sales**. A "Web Page Dialog" box pops up asking if you want to do a quick add of "Cash Sales." Click [ Quick Add ].

3. In the "Sales Date" field, type **10/20/20XX** or use the calendar icon to enter the date.

4. For the "Product/Service," "Quantity," "Rate," "Amount" and Memo" fields, use the following screen as a guide.

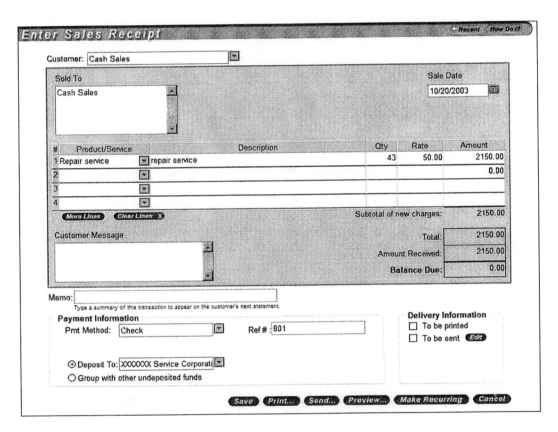

5. Scroll down the "Enter Sales Receipt" screen to complete the following fields.
   a. In the "Pmt Method" field, select "Check."
   b. Type **801** in the "Ref #" field.

c.  In the "Deposit to" field, make sure that "XXXXXXX Service Corporation" appears.

6.  Make sure your screen matches the one shown on previous page, then click [Save].

Now that you have received cash from a cash sale, it is time to learn about making cash payments by writing checks.

**Cash Payments:  Write Checks**

Your business also makes cash payments.  Usually these cash payments are for expenses.  All payments of cash are recorded in the "Write Checks" window.  The transaction you are going to work with is

*Date*              *Transaction*

10/21/20XX    Issued Check No. 4 to Jonathan Brent, a new vendor, for repairs, $75.

Follow these steps to write checks:

1.  Move your mouse over "Banking" on the QuickBooks:  Online Edition menu bar.  When the drop-down menu appears, click on the Write Checks link.  The "Write Checks" screen appears.

2.  Complete the following fields:

Bank Account      "XXXXXXX Service Corporation" is automatically completed.

| | |
|---|---|
| Pay to the Order of | Type **Jonathan Brent**, press <Tab>. In a moment, an "Add Name—Web Page Dialog" box will appear asking if you want to add "Jonathan Brent" and if he is a "Vendor." Click **Quick Add**. |

| | |
|---|---|
| Check # | "4" is automatically displayed. |
| Date | Select "10/21/20XX" |
| Amount | **75.00** (Observe that the check is automatically written.) |
| Memo | Type "Repairs" |
| Account | Either select "Repairs & Maintenance" or add it on the fly. |

3.    Compare your "Write Checks" screen to the one below.

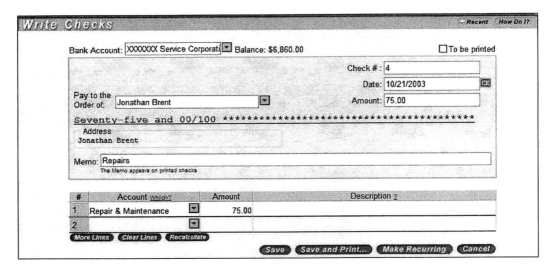

4.    If necessary, make any needed changed. Then click **Save**. A blank "Write Checks" screen appears. Complete the transactions on the next page.

---

| Date | Transaction |
|------|-------------|
| 10/21/20XX | Issued Check No. 5 to the Sun News, a new vendor, for advertising, $125. |
| 10/21/20XX | Issued Check No. 6 to Santa Fe Rentals, a new vendor, for equipment rental, $265.  Use the "Rent or Lease" expense account. |
| 10/22/20XX | Issued Check No. 7 to Comtel, a new vendor, for the monthly telephone and Internet service, $269.  Use the "Office expense" account. |
| 10/30/20XX | Issued Check No. 8 to Regional Utilities, a new vendor, for monthly utilities bill, $206.  Use the "Utilities Expense" account. |
| 10/30/20XX | Issued Check No. 9 to the sole stockholder in payment of a $1,000 cash dividend. Since you are the sole stockholder in your corporation, type **your first and last name** after "Pay to the order of", then **Dividends** in the account field.  Complete the "Mini Interview—Web Page Dialog" boxes to add the Dividends account to your chart of accounts.  Remember Dividends is an "Equity" type of account, its detail type is "Owner's Equity," its description is "cash dividend," and it had a "0" balance as of "10/01/20XX." |

## RECONCILE THE BANK STATEMENT:  OCTOBER

Your business receives a bank statement every month for your regular checking account. The bank statement shows which checks and deposits have cleared the bank.  Use the bank statement below to complete account reconciliation with QuickBooks:  Online Edition.

| REGULAR CHECKING ACCOUNT October 1 - 31, 20XX | | | |
|---|---|---|---|
| Previous Balance | | 2,000.00 | |
| 7 Deposits (+) | | 5,255.00 | |
| 6 checks (-) | | 1,400.00 | |
| Service Charges (-) | 10/31/XX | 25.00 | |
| **Ending Balance** | 10/31/XX | **$5,830.00** | |
| DEPOSITS | | | |
| | 10/14 | 400.00 | |
| | 10/17 | 480.00 | |
| | 10/17 | 95.00 | |
| | 10/17 | 1,050.00 | |
| | 10/19 | 300.00 | |
| | 10/20 | 780.00 | |
| | 10/22 | 2,150.00 | |
| CHECKS (Asterisk * indicates break in check number sequence) | | | |
| 10/15 | 1 | 390.00 | |
| 10/15 | 2 | 300.00 | |
| 10/17 | 3 | 245.00 | |
| 10/29 | 4 | 75.00 | |
| 10/29 | 5 | 125.00 | |
| 10/29 | 6 | 265.00 | |

Follow these steps to reconcile the bank statement.

1. Move your mouse over "Banking" on the QuickBooks: Online Edition menu bar. When the drop-down menu appears, click on Banking Overview. When the "Banking Overview" screen appears, move your mouse over the word "Reconcile" then double click.

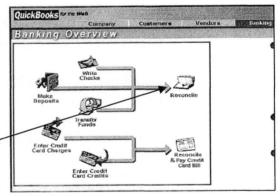

---

Text and screen variations may occur since web-based software products backup and upgrade automatically.

2. A "Choose an account to reconcile -- Web Page Dialog" box appears. Select the account "XXXXXXX Service Corporation" and click [ OK ].

3. A "--Web Page Dialog" box appears. For Question 1 refer to your October bank statement on previous page. Type **10/31/20XX** (your current year) for the "Statement Ending Date," verify the "Opening Balance" is "2000.00" and type **5830.00** as the "Ending Balance."

4. For Question 2 refer to your October bank statement. Type **25.00** for the "Service Charge;" type **10/31/20XX** for the "Date," and select **Bank Charges** for the "Expense Account."

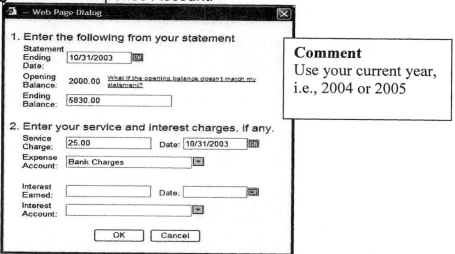

**Comment**
Use your current year, i.e., 2004 or 2005

5. IMPORTANT! Verify that you have entered all information correctly. Errors made when reconciling the bank statement are difficult to correct. Click [ OK ] when you are satisfied.

6. The "Reconcile" screen appears. Click in the "√" column to place a check mark next to each deposit that is shown on your bank statement.

7. Using the bank statement, click in the "√" column to place a check mark next to each check that has cleared your bank. (*Hint: Your company name should show your first and last name Service Corporation.* The screen illustration shows "XXXXXXX Service Corporation" it should show "your name Service Corporation" instead. Your "Num" column may differ. This is okay; the differences are insignificant.)

**Reconcile**

**Account: XXXXXXX  Service Corporation**

1. For every transaction on your statement, click on this screen so a checkmark appears next to it.
2. Use links in Related Activities or navigate using the menus to add missing transactions or make corre
3. When the difference at the bottom equals zero, click Finished. What if it doesn't equal zero?

**Deposits and Other Credits**

| ✓ | Date | Type | Num | Payee | Amount |
|---|------|------|-----|-------|--------|
| ☑ | 10/13/2003 | Payment | 9290 | Two Sisters B&B | 400.00 |
| ☑ | 10/16/2003 | Payment | 4522 | Connections Cafe | 480.00 |
| ☑ | 10/16/2003 | Payment | 816 | Charity Access | 95.00 |
| ☑ | 10/16/2003 | Payment | 9346 | Two Sisters B&B | 1050.00 |
| ☑ | 10/18/2003 | Payment | 901 | Charity Access | 300.00 |
| ☑ | 10/19/2003 | Payment | 5001 | Connections Cafe | 780.00 |
| ☐ | 10/19/2003 | Payment | 9401 | Two Sisters B&B | 540.00 |
| ☑ | 10/20/2003 | Sales Receipt | 801 | Cash Sales | 2150.00 |
| | | | | Total checked(7) amount: | 5255.00 |

**Checks and Payments**                                             Sort by: Date

| ✓ | Date | Type | Num | Payee | Amount |
|---|------|------|-----|-------|--------|
| ☑ | 10/06/2003 | Bill Payment (Check) | 1 | Big Bytes Supplies | 390.00 |
| ☑ | 10/07/2003 | Bill Payment (Check) | 2 | Sales Products Supply | 245.00 |
| ☑ | 10/07/2003 | Bill Payment (Check) | 3 | Big Bytes Supplies | 300.00 |
| ☑ | 10/21/2003 | Check | 4 | Jonathan Brent | 75.00 |
| ☑ | 10/21/2003 | Check | 5 | Sun News | 125.00 |
| ☑ | 10/21/2003 | Check | 6 | Santa Fe Rentals | 265.00 |
| ☐ | 10/22/2003 | Check | 7 | Comtel | 269.00 |
| ☐ | 10/30/2003 | Check | 8 | Regional Utilities | 206.00 |
| ☐ | 10/30/2003 | Check | 9 | Susan Crosson | 1000.00 |
| ☑ | 10/31/2003 | Check | SVCCHRG | | 25.00 |
| | | | | Total checked(7) amount: | 1425.00 |

( Select All ) ( Clear All )

| | | |
|---|---|---|
| Statement Opening Balance: | 2000.00 | |
| Statement Ending Date: | 10/31/2003 | Edit... |
| Statement Ending Balance: | 5830.00 | |
| Cleared Balance: | 5830.00 | |
| Difference: | 0.00 | Make adjusting transaction... |

( Finished ) ( Finish Later ) ( Cancel )

8.   Make sure the "Difference" field shows "0.00." Click ( Finished ). The "Reconcile Report for XXXXXXX Service Corporation" screen appears. Let's learn how to print it.

## PRINTING OCTOBER'S RECONCILATION REPORT

1. The "Reconcile Report for XXXXXXX Service Corporation" screen should be displayed. Make sure that the statement date is 10/31/20XX.

2. Click **Print...**. Your report starts to print.

3. Your "Register Balance as of Reconcile Date" shows 4895.00.

## PRINTING TRANSACTION LIST BY DAY:  OCTOBER

Follow these steps to print the "Transaction List by Date" report.

1. Move your mouse over "Reports" on the QuickBooks: Online Edition menu bar. When the drop-down menu appears, click on All Reports (Report Overview). From the "Accountant & Taxes" list, click on Transaction List by Date.

2. Click **Customize...**. A "Customize Report:  Transaction List—Web Page Dialog" box appears asking about display options, date options, and filter options.

3. Select "Day" for the "Display Options."

4. For "Date Options," select "Custom" for the "Dates." In the "From" box, select "10/01/20XX" as the date. In the "To," box, select "10/31/20XX" as the date.

5. Click **Change Columns...**. Then, remove the Memo/Description column.

6. Click on **Create**

7. Click **Print...**. Make the selections to print in Landscape orientation. Compare your report with the one shown on the next page.

**Report**                                                        🔍 Find Text on Page   How Do I?

Print...  Email...  Excel...  Customize...  ⟳ Memorize...

## XXXXXXX Service Corporation
## Transaction List by Date
### October 2003

| Date | Type | Num | Name | Account | Split | Amount |
|---|---|---|---|---|---|---|
| 10/01/2003 | Deposit | | | XXXXXXX Service Corporation | Paid in Capital | 2000.00 |
| 10/01/2003 | General Journal | | | | -SPLIT- | |
| 10/01/2003 | Deposit | | | Prepaid Insurance | Paid in Capital | 200.00 |
| 10/01/2003 | General Journal | | | | -SPLIT- | |
| 10/01/2003 | Invoice | 1001 | Two Sisters B&B | Accounts Receivable | Services | 400.00 |
| 10/01/2003 | Invoice | 1002 | Connections Cafe | Accounts Receivable | Services | 480.00 |
| 10/01/2003 | Invoice | 1003 | Charity Access | Accounts Receivable | Services | 95.00 |
| 10/01/2003 | Bill | | Big Bytes Supplies | Accounts Payable | Other Miscellaneous Expense | 440.00 |
| 10/01/2003 | Bill | | Sales Products Supply | Accounts Payable | Other Miscellaneous Expense | 200.00 |
| 10/02/2003 | Bill | 66JE | Big Bytes Supplies | Accounts Payable | Computer Supplies | 300.00 |
| 10/03/2003 | Bill | EX32 | Sales Products Supply | Accounts Payable | Office Expenses | 245.00 |
| 10/04/2003 | Bill | 89JE | Big Bytes Supplies | Accounts Payable | Computer Supplies | 520.00 |
| 10/05/2003 | Bill | EX45 | Sales Products Supply | Accounts Payable | Office Expenses | 385.00 |
| 10/05/2003 | Vendor Credit | 66JE | Big Bytes Supplies | Accounts Payable | Computer Supplies | -50.00 |
| 10/06/2003 | Bill Payment (Check) | 1 | Big Bytes Supplies | XXXXXXX Service Corporation | -SPLIT- | -390.00 |
| 10/07/2003 | Bill Payment (Check) | 2 | Sales Products Supply | XXXXXXX Service Corporation | Accounts Payable | -245.00 |
| 10/07/2003 | Bill Payment (Check) | 3 | Big Bytes Supplies | XXXXXXX Service Corporation | Accounts Payable | -300.00 |
| 10/08/2003 | Invoice | 1004 | Two Sisters B&B | Accounts Receivable | Services | 1200.00 |
| 10/09/2003 | Invoice | 1005 | Charity Access | Accounts Receivable | Services | 300.00 |
| 10/10/2003 | Invoice | 1006 | Connections Cafe | Accounts Receivable | -SPLIT- | 780.00 |
| 10/11/2003 | Invoice | 1007 | Two Sisters B&B | Accounts Receivable | -SPLIT- | 540.00 |
| 10/13/2003 | Credit Memo | 1008 | Two Sisters B&B | Accounts Receivable | Services | -150.00 |
| 10/13/2003 | Payment | 9290 | Two Sisters B&B | XXXXXXX Service Corporation | -SPLIT- | 400.00 |
| 10/16/2003 | Payment | 4522 | Connections Cafe | XXXXXXX Service Corporation | Accounts Receivable | 480.00 |
| 10/16/2003 | Payment | 816 | Charity Access | XXXXXXX Service Corporation | Accounts Receivable | 95.00 |
| 10/16/2003 | Payment | 9346 | Two Sisters B&B | XXXXXXX Service Corporation | Accounts Receivable | 1050.00 |
| 10/18/2003 | Payment | 901 | Charity Access | XXXXXXX Service Corporation | Accounts Receivable | 300.00 |
| 10/19/2003 | Payment | 5001 | Connections Cafe | XXXXXXX Service Corporation | Accounts Receivable | 780.00 |
| 10/19/2003 | Payment | 9401 | Two Sisters B&B | XXXXXXX Service Corporation | Accounts Receivable | 540.00 |
| 10/20/2003 | Sales Receipt | 1009 | Cash Sales | XXXXXXX Service Corporation | Services | 2150.00 |
| 10/21/2003 | Check | 4 | Jonathan Brent | XXXXXXX Service Corporation | Repair and Maintenance | -75.00 |
| 10/21/2003 | Check | 5 | Sun News | XXXXXXX Service Corporation | Advertising | -125.00 |
| 10/21/2003 | Check | 6 | Santa Fe Rentals | XXXXXXX Service Corporation | Rent or Lease | -265.00 |
| 10/22/2003 | Check | 7 | Comtel | XXXXXXX Service Corporation | Office Expenses | -269.00 |
| 10/30/2003 | Check | 8 | Regional Utilities | XXXXXXX Service Corporation | Utilities | -206.00 |
| 10/30/2003 | Check | 9 | Susan Crosson | XXXXXXX Service Corporation | Dividends | -1000.00 |
| 10/31/2003 | Check | SVCCHRG | | XXXXXXX Service Corporation | Bank Charges | -25.00 |

Text and screen variations may occur since web-based software products backup and upgrade automatically.

## PRINTING OCTOBER'S TRIAL BALANCE

1. Move your mouse over "Reports" on the QuickBooks: Online Edition menu bar. When the drop-down menu appears, click on All Reports (Report Overview). Scroll down to the "Accountant & Taxes" list and link to <u>Trial Balance</u>.

2. Click **Customize...**. In a few moments, a "Customize Report: Trial Balance—Web Page Dialog" box appears asking about display options and date options.

3. For "Display Options," select "Accrual" by clicking on its radio button.

4. For "Date Options," select "Custom" for "Dates." Make sure the "From" date is "10/01/20XX" and the "To" date displays "10/31/20XX."

5. Click **Create**.

> **Comment**
> Current Year, i.e., 2004 or 2005

### XXXXXXX Service Corporation
### Trial Balance
As of October 31, 2003

| | Debit | Credit |
|---|---|---|
| XXXXXXX Service Corporation | 4,895.00 | |
| Accounts Receivable | 0.00 | |
| Prepaid Insurance | 200.00 | |
| Computer Equipment:Accumulated Depreciation | | 1,200.00 |
| Computer Equipment:Original Cost | 6,000.00 | |
| Accounts Payable | | 1,105.00 |
| Common Stock | | 1,000.00 |
| Dividends | 1,000.00 | |
| Paid in Capital | | 6,000.00 |
| Services | | 5,795.00 |
| Advertising | 125.00 | |
| Bank Charges | 25.00 | |
| Computer Supplies | 770.00 | |
| Office Expenses | 899.00 | |
| Rent or Lease | 265.00 | |
| Repair and Maintenance | 75.00 | |
| Utilities | 206.00 | |
| Other Miscellaneous Expense | 640.00 | |
| TOTAL | $15,100.00 | $15,100.00 |

## EDITING THE OCTOBER 31 TRIAL BALANCE

Observe that your trial balance shows a 640.00 balance in the "Other miscellaneous expense account." This is because QuickBooks Online recorded the opening balance for Big Bytes Supplies and Sales Products Supply in this account: $440 (Big Bytes Supplies) + $200 (Sales Products Supply = $640.00.

Follow these steps to change this default to the appropriate accounts.

1. Place your mouse over 640.00. Double-click on 640.00.

2. Notice that the two vendors are listed: Big Bytes Supplies and Sales Products Supply. Link to each vendor. Then edit the information in the Account field as follows:

   Big Bytes Supplies:      Computer Supplies – Expense
   Sales Products Supply:   Office Expense

3. Save each change. Then print your 10/01/20XX to 10/31/20XX trial balance. Compare it to the one shown below.

**XXXXXX Service Corporation**
**Trial Balance**
As of October 31, 2003

| | Debit | Credit |
|---|---|---|
| XXXXXX Service Corporation | 4,895.00 | |
| Accounts Receivable | 0.00 | |
| Prepaid Insurance | 200.00 | |
| Computer Equipment:Accumulated Depreciation | | 1,200.00 |
| Computer Equipment:Original Cost | 6,000.00 | |
| Accounts Payable | | 1,105.00 |
| Common Stock | | 1,000.00 |
| Dividends | 1,000.00 | |
| Paid in Capital | | 6,000.00 |
| Retained Earnings | | 0.00 |
| Services | | 5,795.00 |
| Advertising | 125.00 | |
| Bank Charges | 25.00 | |
| Computer Supplies | 1,210.00 | |
| Office Expenses | 1,099.00 | |
| Rent or Lease | 265.00 | |
| Repair & Maintenance | 75.00 | |
| Utilities | 206.00 | |
| TOTAL | $15,100.00 | $15,100.00 |

## PRINTING OCTOBER'S INCOME STATEMENT

1. Move your mouse over "Reports" on the QuickBooks: Online Edition menu bar. When the drop-down menu appears, click on Profit & Loss (what QuickBooks calls the Income Statement).

2. Click **Customize...**. In a few moments, a "Customize Report: Profit & Loss—Web Page Dialog" box appears asking about display options and date options.

3. For "Display Options," select "Accrual" by clicking on its radio button.

4. For "Date Options," select "Custom" for "Dates." Make sure the "From" date is "10/01/20XX" and the "To" date displays "10/31/20XX."

5. Click **Create**.

6. Click **Print...**.

## XXXXXXX Service Corporation
### Profit & Loss
#### October 2003

|  | Total |
|---|---|
| **Income** |  |
| Services | 5,795.00 |
| **Total Income** | **$5,795.00** |
| **Expenses** |  |
| Advertising | 125.00 |
| Bank Charges | 25.00 |
| Computer Supplies | 1,210.00 |
| Office Expenses | 1,099.00 |
| Rent or Lease | 265.00 |
| Repair & Maintenance | 75.00 |
| Utilities | 206.00 |
| **Total Expenses** | **$3,005.00** |
| **Net Operating Income** | **$2,790.00** |
| **Net Income** | **$2,790.00** |

---

## PRINTING OCTOBER'S BALANCE SHEET

1. Move your mouse over "Reports" on the QuickBooks: Online Edition menu bar. When the drop-down menu appears, click on Balance Sheet.

2. Click **Customize...**. In a few moments, a "Customize Report: Balance Sheet—Web Page Dialog" box appears asking about display options and date options.

3. For "Display Options," select "Accrual" by clicking on its radio button.

4. For "Date Options," select "Custom" for "Dates." Make sure the "From" date is "10/01/20XX" and the "To" date displays "10/31/20XX."

5. Click **Create**.

6. Click **Print...**. Compare your printout to the one shown on the next page.

---

**XXXXXXX Service Corporation**
**Balance Sheet**
As of October 31, 2003

| | Total |
|---|---|
| **ASSETS** | |
| Current Assets | |
| Bank Accounts | |
| XXXXXXX Service Corporation | 4,895.00 |
| Total Bank Accounts | $4,895.00 |
| Accounts Receivable | |
| Accounts Receivable | 0.00 |
| Total Accounts Receivable | $0.00 |
| Other Current Assets | |
| Prepaid Insurance | 200.00 |
| Total Other Current Assets | $200.00 |
| Total Current Assets | $5,095.00 |
| Fixed Assets | |
| Computer Equipment | |
| Accumulated Depreciation | -1,200.00 |
| Original Cost | 6,000.00 |
| Total Computer Equipment | $4,800.00 |
| Total Fixed Assets | $4,800.00 |
| TOTAL ASSETS | $9,895.00 |
| **LIABILITIES AND EQUITY** | |
| Liabilities | |
| Current Liabilities | |
| Accounts Payable | |
| Accounts Payable | 1,105.00 |
| Total Accounts Payable | $1,105.00 |
| Total Current Liabilities | $1,105.00 |
| Total Liabilities | $1,105.00 |
| Equity | |
| Common Stock | 1,000.00 |
| Dividends | -1,000.00 |
| Paid in Capital | 6,000.00 |
| Retained Earnings | 0.00 |
| Net Income | 2,790.00 |
| Total Equity | $8,790.00 |
| TOTAL LIABILITIES AND EQUITY | $9,895.00 |

**7.** Log off or continue.

## NOVEMBER TRANSACTIONS

Complete the following transactions for November.

*Date*   *Transaction*

11/02/20XX   Pay vendor bill. Issued Check No. 10 to the Sales Products Supply in payment of Invoice EX45, $385.

11/04/20XX   Enter vendor bill. Received Invoice 98JE and shipment from Big Bytes Supplies for the purchase of computer supplies on credit, Net 30, $2,625.

11/04/20XX   Received Invoice EX55 and shipment from Sales Products Supply for the purchase of office supplies on credit, Net 30, $875.

11/05/20XX   Paid vendor bill. Paid Sales Products Supply the 10/01/20XX $200 opening balance with hand-written Check No. 11.

11/05/20XX   Paid Big Bytes Supplies, Invoice 89JE, for the October 4 purchase, $520.00, hand-written Check No. 12.

11/06/20XX   Paid Big Bytes Supplies, Invoice 98JE, for the November 4 purchase, $2,625.00, hand-written Check No. 13.

11/07/20XX   Paid Sales Products Supply, Invoice EX55, for the November 4 purchase, $875.00, Check No. 14.

11/8/20XX   Create invoice. Sold maintenance services on account to Two Sisters B&B, Invoice, Net 30, $1,500 for 50 hours of maintenance services at $30 an hour. (Hint: Delivery Information, uncheck "To be printed.")

11/8/20XX   Sold maintenance services on account to Connections Cafe, Invoice, Net 30, $1,560 for 52 hours of maintenance at $30 an hour.

| | |
|---|---|
| 11/17/20XX | Receive payment. Received a check from Connections Cafe in payment of Invoice, $1560.00, Check No. 5110. |
| 11/17/20XX | Received a check from Two Sisters B&B in payment of Invoice, $1,500.00, Check No. 221. |
| 11/21/20XX | Enter sales receipt. Cash sales $2,300, payment received by Check No. 802 for 46 hours of repair services at $50 an hour. (Hint: Delivery Information, uncheck "To be printed.") |
| 11/29/20XX | Write Check No. 15 to Comtel from bank account for the monthly telephone and Internet service, $270.00. |
| 11/29/20XX | Write Check No. 16 to Regional Utilities for monthly utilities bill, $210.00. |
| 11/29/20XX | Write Check No. 17 for a cash dividend to the sole stockholder (you), $1,000 from checking account. |

## RECONCILE THE BANK STATEMENT: NOVEMBER

Your business receives a bank statement every month for your regular checking account. The bank statement shows that checks and deposits have cleared the bank. Use the bank statement on the next page to complete account reconciliation for November.

| REGULAR CHECKING ACCOUNT November 1 - 30, 20XX | | | |
|---|---|---|---|
| Previous Balance | | $5,830.00 | |
| 4 Deposits (+) | | 5,900.00 | |
| 9 checks (-) | | 6,350.00 | |
| Service Charges (-) | 11/30/XX | 25.00 | |
| **Ending Balance** | 11/30/XX | **$5,355.00** | |
| DEPOSITS | | | |
| | 11/02 | 540.00 | |
| | 11/18 | 1,560.00 | |
| | 11/20 | 1,500.00 | |
| | 11/22 | 2,300.00 | |
| CHECKS (Asterisk * indicates break in check number sequence) | | | |
| 11/02 | 7 | 269.00 | |
| 11/02 | 8 | 206.00 | |
| 11/03 | 9 | 1,000.00 | |
| 11/04 | 10 | 385.00 | |
| 110/6 | 11 | 200.00 | |
| 11/06 | 12 | 520.00 | |
| 11/08 | 13 | 2,625.00 | |
| 11/08 | 14 | 875.00 | |
| 11/23 | 15 | 270.00 | |

From the "Banking" drop-down menu on the QuickBooks:  Online Edition menu bar, go to the link for <u>Reconcile</u>.   Complete the steps for reconciling your November bank statement.  Then, compare your Reconciliation Summary to the one shown on the next page.

---

**Comment:**
If a check or deposit does *not* appear on your "Reconcile" screen, click on the appropriate link on the QuickBooks: Online Edition menu bar.  Select the "Edit" button and make any needed corrections.  To update the record, click on "Save."

---

## November's Reconciliation Summary

**XXXXXXX Service Corporation**
**Reconcile Report for XXXXXXX Service Corporation**
This is a static report. Any changes to transactions since the reconcile date are not reflected here.
Report created on 07/27/2003.

Account: XXXXXX Service Corporation
Statement Date: 11/30/2003
Reconcile Date: 07/27/2003

**Summary**

| | |
|---|---|
| Opening Balance | 5830.00 |
| Ending Balance of Statement | 5355.00 |
| Uncleared Amount | -1210.00 |
| Register Balance as of Reconcile Date | 4145.00 |

**Cleared Transactions**

| Date | Type | Num | Payee | Amount |
|---|---|---|---|---|
| **Cleared Checks and Payments** | | | | |
| 10/22/2003 | Check | 7 | Comtel | 269.00 |
| 10/30/2003 | Check | 8 | Regional Utilities | 206.00 |
| 10/30/2003 | Check | 9 | XXXXXXX | 1000.00 |
| 11/02/2003 | Bill Pmt | 10 | Sales Products Supply | 385.00 |
| 11/05/2003 | Bill Pmt | 11 | Sales Products Supply | 200.00 |
| 11/05/2003 | Bill Pmt | 12 | Big Bytes Supplies | 520.00 |
| 11/06/2003 | Bill Pmt | 13 | Big Bytes Supplies | 2625.00 |
| 11/07/2003 | Bill Pmt | 14 | Sales Products Supply | 875.00 |
| 11/29/2003 | Check | 15 | Comtel | 270.00 |
| 11/30/2003 | Check | SVCCHRG | | 25.00 |
| | | | | Subtotal: 6375.00 |
| **Cleared Deposits and Other Credits** | | | | |
| 10/19/2003 | Payment | 9401 | Two Sisters B&B | 540.00 |
| 11/17/2003 | Payment | 5110 | Connections Cafe | 1560.00 |
| 11/17/2003 | Payment | 221 | Two Sisters B&B | 1500.00 |
| 11/21/2003 | Sales Receipt | 802 | Cash Sales | 2300.00 |
| | | | | Subtotal: 5900.00 |

**Total Cleared Transactions**                                                         -475.00

**Uncleared Transactions as of 11/30/2003**

| Date | Type | Num | Payee | Amount |
|---|---|---|---|---|
| **Uncleared Checks and Payments** | | | | |
| 11/29/2003 | Check | 16 | Regional Utilities | 210.00 |
| 11/29/2003 | Check | 17 | XXXXXXX | 1000.00 |
| | | | | Subtotal: 1210.00 |

## PRINTING NOVEMBER REPORTS

1. Print "Transaction List by Day" report for November 1, 20XX through November 30, 20XX. Compare your report to the one shown on page 123. (Hints: Click on Change columns—remove "Memo/Description." For Rows/Columns--select "Day" from the pull-down menu.)

2. Print the November 30, 20XX trial balance. Compare your report to the one shown on page 124.

3. Print the October 1, 20XX through November 30, 20XX income statement. Compare your report to the one shown on page 125.

4. Print the November 30, 20XX balance sheet. Compare your report to the one shown on page 126.

## November Transaction List by Day

Report       How Do I?

Print... Email... Excel... Customize... Memorize...

**XXXXXXX Service Corporation**
**Transaction List by Day**
November 2003

| Date | Type | Num | Name | Account | Split | Amount |
|---|---|---|---|---|---|---|
| **November 2, 2003** | | | | | | |
| 11/02/2003 | Bill Payment (Check) | 10 | Sales Products Supply | XXXXXXX Service Corporation | Accounts Payable | -385.00 |
| Total for November 2, 2003 | | | | | | $ -385.00 |
| **November 4, 2003** | | | | | | |
| 11/04/2003 | Bill | 98JE | Big Bytes Supplies | Accounts Payable | Computer Supplies | 2625.00 |
| 11/04/2003 | Bill | EX55 | Sales Products Supply | Accounts Payable | Office Expenses | 875.00 |
| Total for November 4, 2003 | | | | | | $3,500.00 |
| **November 5, 2003** | | | | | | |
| 11/05/2003 | Bill Payment (Check) | 11 | Sales Products Supply | XXXXXXX Service Corporation | Accounts Payable | -200.00 |
| 11/05/2003 | Bill Payment (Check) | 12 | Big Bytes Supplies | XXXXXXX Service Corporation | Accounts Payable | -520.00 |
| Total for November 5, 2003 | | | | | | $ -720.00 |
| **November 6, 2003** | | | | | | |
| 11/06/2003 | Bill Payment (Check) | 13 | Big Bytes Supplies | XXXXXXX Service Corporation | Accounts Payable | -2625.00 |
| Total for November 6, 2003 | | | | | | $ -2,625.00 |
| **November 7, 2003** | | | | | | |
| 11/07/2003 | Bill Payment (Check) | 14 | Sales Products Supply | XXXXXXX Service Corporation | Accounts Payable | -875.00 |
| Total for November 7, 2003 | | | | | | $ -875.00 |
| **November 8, 2003** | | | | | | |
| 11/08/2003 | Invoice | 1012 | Two Sisters B&B | Accounts Receivable | Services | 1500.00 |
| 11/08/2003 | Invoice | 1013 | Connections Cafe | Accounts Receivable | Services | 1560.00 |
| Total for November 8, 2003 | | | | | | $3,060.00 |
| **November 17, 2003** | | | | | | |
| 11/17/2003 | Payment | 5110 | Connections Cafe | XXXXXXX Service Corporation | Accounts Receivable | 1560.00 |
| 11/17/2003 | Payment | 221 | Two Sisters B&B | XXXXXXX Service Corporation | Accounts Receivable | 1500.00 |
| Total for November 17, 2003 | | | | | | $3,060.00 |
| **November 21, 2003** | | | | | | |
| 11/21/2003 | Sales Receipt | 1014 | Cash Sales | XXXXXXX Service Corporation | Services | 2300.00 |
| Total for November 21, 2003 | | | | | | $2,300.00 |
| **November 29, 2003** | | | | | | |
| 11/29/2003 | Check | 15 | Comtel | XXXXXXX Service Corporation | Office Expenses | -270.00 |
| 11/29/2003 | Check | 16 | Regional Utilities | XXXXXXX Service Corporation | Utilities | -210.00 |
| 11/29/2003 | Check | 17 | XXXXXXX | XXXXXXX Service Corporation | Dividends | -1000.00 |
| Total for November 29, 2003 | | | | | | $ -1,480.00 |
| **November 30, 2003** | | | | | | |
| 11/30/2003 | Check | SVCCHRG | | XXXXXXX Service Corporation | Bank Charges | -25.00 |
| Total for November 30, 2003 | | | | | | $ -25.00 |

## November Trial Balance

**XXXXXXX Service Corporation**
**Trial Balance**
As of November 30, 2003

| | Debit | Credit |
|---|---|---|
| XXXXXXX Service Corporation | 4,145.00 | |
| Accounts Receivable | 0.00 | |
| Prepaid Insurance | 200.00 | |
| Computer Equipment:Accumulated Depreciation | | 1,200.00 |
| Computer Equipment:Original Cost | 6,000.00 | |
| Accounts Payable | | 0.00 |
| Common Stock | | 1,000.00 |
| Dividends | 2,000.00 | |
| Paid in Capital | | 6,000.00 |
| Services | | 11,155.00 |
| Advertising | 125.00 | |
| Bank Charges | 50.00 | |
| Computer Supplies | 3,835.00 | |
| Office Expenses | 2,244.00 | |
| Rent or Lease | 265.00 | |
| Repair & Maintenance | 75.00 | |
| Utilities | 416.00 | |
| TOTAL | $19,355.00 | $19,355.00 |

**November Income Statement**

## XXXXXXX Service Corporation
## Profit & Loss
### October - November, 2003

|  | Total |
|---|---|
| **Income** | |
| Services | 11,155.00 |
| **Total Income** | **$11,155.00** |
| **Expenses** | |
| Advertising | 125.00 |
| Bank Charges | 50.00 |
| Computer Supplies | 3,835.00 |
| Office Expenses | 2,244.00 |
| Rent or Lease | 265.00 |
| Repair & Maintenance | 75.00 |
| Utilities | 416.00 |
| **Total Expenses** | **$7,010.00** |
| **Net Operating Income** | **$4,145.00** |
| **Net Income** | **$4,145.00** |

**Comment:**

QuickBooks: Online Edition uses the title "Profit & Loss" to refer to the income statement. The income statement is where business reports its revenues and expenses and determines its net income or loss for the period.

## November Balance Sheet

**XXXXXXX Service Corporation**
**Balance Sheet**
As of November 30, 2003

| | Total |
|---|---|
| **ASSETS** | |
| Current Assets | |
| Bank Accounts | |
| XXXXXXX Service Corporation | 4,145.00 |
| Total Bank Accounts | $4,145.00 |
| Accounts Receivable | |
| Accounts Receivable | 0.00 |
| Total Accounts Receivable | $0.00 |
| Other Current Assets | |
| Prepaid Insurance | 200.00 |
| Total Other Current Assets | $200.00 |
| Total Current Assets | $4,345.00 |
| Fixed Assets | |
| Computer Equipment | |
| Accumulated Depreciation | -1,200.00 |
| Original Cost | 6,000.00 |
| Total Computer Equipment | $4,800.00 |
| Total Fixed Assets | $4,800.00 |
| **TOTAL ASSETS** | $9,145.00 |
| **LIABILITIES AND EQUITY** | |
| Liabilities | |
| Current Liabilities | |
| Accounts Payable | |
| Accounts Payable | 0.00 |
| Total Accounts Payable | $0.00 |
| Total Current Liabilities | $0.00 |
| Total Liabilities | $0.00 |
| Equity | |
| Common Stock | 1,000.00 |
| Dividends | -2,000.00 |
| Paid In Capital | 6,000.00 |
| Retained Earnings | 0.00 |
| Net Income | 4,145.00 |
| Total Equity | $9,145.00 |
| **TOTAL LIABILITIES AND EQUITY** | $9,145.00 |

Text and screen variations may occur since web-based software products backup and upgrade automatically.

## DECEMBER TRANSACTIONS

Complete the following transactions for December.

| *Date* | *Transaction* |
|---|---|
| ✓12/02/20XX | Write Check No. 18 to Pro Insurance, a new vendor, in payment of next year's insurance premiums, $210. *(Hint: Use the "Prepaid insurance" account.)* |
| ✓12/02/20XX | Received vendor bill. Invoice 113JE and shipment from Big Bytes Supplies for the purchase of computer supplies on credit, Net 30, $2,050. |
| ✓12/03/20XX | Received Invoice EX82 and shipment from Sales Products Supply for the purchase of office supplies on credit, Net 30, $700. |
| ✓12/08/20XX | Create invoice. Sold repair and maintenance services on account to Two Sisters B & B, Invoice Net 30, $1,800 for 30 hours of repairs and 10 hours of maintenance. (Hint: Delivery Information, uncheck "To be printed.") |
| ✓12/08/20XX | Sold repair and maintenance services on account to Connections Cafe, Invoice Net 30, $970 for 14 hours of repairs and 9 hours of maintenance. |
| ✓12/09/20XX | Sold 10 hours of maintenance services on account to the Charity Access, Invoice Net 30, for a total of $300. |
| ✓12/10/20XX | Sold 4 hours of repair services on account to Charity Access, Invoice Net 30, for a total of $200. |
| ✓12/11/20XX | Vendor bill paid to Big Bytes Supplies, Invoice 113JE for the December 2 purchase, $2,050.00, hand-written Check No. 19. |

| | |
|---|---|
| 12/11/20XX | Paid Sales Products Supply, Invoice EX82, for the December 3 purchase, $700.00, hand-written Check No. 20. |
| 12/17/20XX | Received customer payment. Received a check from Connections Cafe in payment of Invoice, $970, Check No. 5225. |
| 12/17/20XX | Received a check from Two Sisters B & B in payment of Invoice, $1,800, Check No. 301. |
| 12/19/20XX | Received a check from Charity Access in payment of Invoices, $500, Check No. 935. |
| 12/24/20XX | Entered sales receipt. Cash sales $2,200, received check No. 803 for 44 hours of repair services. (Hint: Delivery Information, uncheck "To be printed.") |
| 12/30/20XX | Write Check No. 21 to Comtel for monthly telephone and Internet service, $303. |
| 12/30/20XX | Write Check No. 22 to Regional Utilities for monthly utilities bill, $190. |
| 12/30/20XX | Write Check No. 23 to Sun News for advertising $145. |
| 12/30/20XX | Write Check No. 24 to Jonathan Brent for repairs $140. |

---

**Remember:**
Uncheck "To be printed" in the Delivery Information box each time you create an invoice (credit sales) or enter a sales receipt (cash sales).

---

## RECONCILE THE BANK STATEMENT:  DECEMBER

You business receives a bank statement every month for your regular checking account. The bank statement shows that checks and deposits have cleared the bank.  Use the bank statement below to complete account reconciliation for December.

| REGULAR CHECKING ACCOUNT December 1 - 31, 20XX | | | |
|---|---|---|---|
| Previous Balance | | $5,355.00 | |
| 4Deposits (+) | | 5,470.00 | |
| 5checks (-) | | 4,170.00 | |
| Service Charges (-) | 12/31/XX | 25.00 | |
| **Ending Balance** | 12/31/XX | $6,630.00 | |
| DEPOSITS | | | |
| | 12/18 | 970.00 | |
| | 12/19 | 1,800.00 | |
| | 12/20 | 500.00 | |
| | 12/26 | 2,200.00 | |
| CHECKS (Asterisk * indicates break in check number sequence) | | | |
| 12/5 | 16 | 210.00 | |
| 12/5 | 17 | 1,000.00 | |
| 12/7 | 18 | 210.00 | |
| 12/15 | 19 | 2,050.00 | |
| 12/18 | 20 | 700.00 | |

From the "Banking" drop-down menu, go to the link for <u>Reconcile</u>. Complete the steps for reconciling your December bank statement. Then, compare your Reconciliation Summary to the one shown on the next page.

---

**Comment:**
If a check or deposit does *not* appear on your "Reconcile" screen, click on the "Transactions" tab.  Then, select the appropriate link.  Select the "Edit" button and make any needed corrections.  To update the record, click on "Submit."

---

## December's Reconciliation Summary

**XXXXXXX Service Corporation**
**Reconcile Report for XXXXXXX Service Corporation**
This is a static report. Any changes to transactions since the reconcile date are not reflected here.
Report created on 07/28/2003.

Account: XXXXXXX Service Corporation
Statement Date: 12/31/2003
Reconcile Date: 07/28/2003

**Summary**

| | |
|---|---|
| Opening Balance | 5355.00 |
| Ending Balance of Statement | 6630.00 |
| Uncleared Amount | -778.00 |
| Register Balance as of Reconcile Date | 5852.00 |

**Cleared Transactions**

| Date | Type | Num | Payee | Amount |
|---|---|---|---|---|
| **Cleared Checks and Payments** | | | | |
| 11/29/2003 | Check | 16 | Regional Utilities | 210.00 |
| 11/29/2003 | Check | 17 | XXXXXXX | 1000.00 |
| 12/02/2003 | Check | 18 | Pro Insurance | 210.00 |
| 12/11/2003 | Bill Pmt | 19 | Big Bytes Supplies | 2050.00 |
| 12/11/2003 | Bill Pmt | 20 | Sales Products Supply | 700.00 |
| 12/31/2003 | Check | SVCCHRG | | 25.00 |
| | | | | Subtotal: 4195.00 |
| **Cleared Deposits and Other Credits** | | | | |
| 12/17/2003 | Payment | 5225 | Connections Cafe | 970.00 |
| 12/17/2003 | Payment | 301 | Two Sisters B&B | 1800.00 |
| 12/19/2003 | Payment | 935 | Charity Access | 500.00 |
| 12/24/2003 | Sales Receipt | 803 | Cash Sales | 2200.00 |
| | | | | Subtotal: 5470.00 |

**Total Cleared Transactions**    1275.00

**Uncleared Transactions as of 12/31/2003**

| Date | Type | Num | Payee | Amount |
|---|---|---|---|---|
| **Uncleared Checks and Payments** | | | | |
| 12/30/2003 | Check | 21 | Comtel | 303.00 |
| 12/30/2003 | Check | 22 | Regional Utilities | 190.00 |
| 12/30/2003 | Check | 23 | Sun News | 145.00 |
| 12/30/2003 | Check | 24 | Jonathan Brent | 140.00 |
| | | | | Subtotal: 778.00 |
| **Uncleared Deposits and Other Credits** | | | | |
| | | | | Subtotal: 0.00 |

Text and screen variations may occur since web-based software products backup and upgrade automatically.

## PRINTING DECEMBER REPORTS

Print the following reports and compare them to the ones shown on pages 132 - 135.

1.  Print the "Transaction List by Day" report for December 1, 20XX through December 31, 20XX.  Compare your report to the one shown on page132.  (Hints: Click on Change columns—remove "Memo/Description."   For Rows/Columns--select "Day" from the pull-down menu.)

2.  Print the December 31, 20XX trial balance.  Compare your report to the one shown on page 133.

3.  Print the October 1, 20XX through December 31, 20XX income statement.  Compare your report to the one shown on page 134.

4.  Print the December 31, 20XX balance sheet.  Compare your report to the one shown on page 135.

## December's Transaction List by Day

### XXXXXXX Service Corporation
### Transaction List by Day
#### December 2003

| Date | Type | Num | Name | Account | Split | Amount |
|------|------|-----|------|---------|-------|--------|
| **December 2, 2003** | | | | | | |
| 12/02/2003 | Check | 18 | Pro Insurance | XXXXXXX Service Corporation | Prepaid Insurance | -210.00 |
| 12/02/2003 | Bill | 113JE | Big Bytes Supplies | Accounts Payable | Computer Supplies | 2050.00 |
| Total for December 2, 2003 | | | | | | $1,840.00 |
| **December 3, 2003** | | | | | | |
| 12/03/2003 | Bill | EX82 | Sales Products Supply | Accounts Payable | Office Expenses | 700.00 |
| Total for December 3, 2003 | | | | | | $700.00 |
| **December 8, 2003** | | | | | | |
| 12/08/2003 | Invoice | 1015 | Two Sisters B&B | Accounts Receivable | -SPLIT- | 1800.00 |
| 12/08/2003 | Invoice | 1016 | Connections Cafe | Accounts Receivable | -SPLIT- | 970.00 |
| Total for December 8, 2003 | | | | | | $2,770.00 |
| **December 9, 2003** | | | | | | |
| 12/09/2003 | Invoice | 1017 | Charity Access | Accounts Receivable | Services | 300.00 |
| Total for December 9, 2003 | | | | | | $300.00 |
| **December 10, 2003** | | | | | | |
| 12/10/2003 | Invoice | 1018 | Charity Access | Accounts Receivable | Services | 200.00 |
| Total for December 10, 2003 | | | | | | $200.00 |
| **December 11, 2003** | | | | | | |
| 12/11/2003 | Bill Payment (Check) | 19 | Big Bytes Supplies | XXXXXXX Service Corporation | Accounts Payable | -2050.00 |
| 12/11/2003 | Bill Payment (Check) | 20 | Sales Products Supply | XXXXXXX Service Corporation | Accounts Payable | -700.00 |
| Total for December 11, 2003 | | | | | | $ -2,750.00 |
| **December 17, 2003** | | | | | | |
| 12/17/2003 | Payment | 5225 | Connections Cafe | XXXXXXX Service Corporation | Accounts Receivable | 970.00 |
| 12/17/2003 | Payment | 301 | Two Sisters B&B | XXXXXXX Service Corporation | Accounts Receivable | 1800.00 |
| Total for December 17, 2003 | | | | | | $2,770.00 |
| **December 19, 2003** | | | | | | |
| 12/19/2003 | Payment | 935 | Charity Access | XXXXXXX Service Corporation | Accounts Receivable | 500.00 |
| Total for December 19, 2003 | | | | | | $500.00 |
| **December 24, 2003** | | | | | | |
| 12/24/2003 | Sales Receipt | 1019 | Cash Sales | XXXXXXX Service Corporation | Services | 2200.00 |
| Total for December 24, 2003 | | | | | | $2,200.00 |
| **December 30, 2003** | | | | | | |
| 12/30/2003 | Check | 21 | Comtel | XXXXXXX Service Corporation | Office Expenses | -303.00 |
| 12/30/2003 | Check | 22 | Regional Utilities | XXXXXXX Service Corporation | Utilities | -190.00 |
| 12/30/2003 | Check | 23 | Sun News | XXXXXXX Service Corporation | Advertising | -145.00 |
| 12/30/2003 | Check | 24 | Jonathan Brent | XXXXXXX Service Corporation | Repair & Maintenance | -140.00 |
| Total for December 30, 2003 | | | | | | $ -778.00 |
| **December 31, 2003** | | | | | | |
| 12/31/2003 | Check | SVCCHRG | | XXXXXXX Service Corporation | Bank Charges | -25.00 |
| Total for December 31, 2003 | | | | | | $ -25.00 |

Text and screen variations may occur since web-based software products backup and upgrade automatically.

## December's Trial Balance

**XXXXXX Service Corporation**
**Trial Balance**
As of December 31, 2003

| | Debit | Credit |
|---|---|---|
| XXXXXX Service Corporation | 5,852.00 | |
| Accounts Receivable | 0.00 | |
| Prepaid Insurance | 410.00 | |
| Computer Equipment:Accumulated Depreciation | | 1,200.00 |
| Computer Equipment:Original Cost | 6,000.00 | |
| Accounts Payable | | 0.00 |
| Common Stock | | 1,000.00 |
| Dividends | 2,000.00 | |
| Paid in Capital | | 6,000.00 |
| Services | | 16,625.00 |
| Advertising | 270.00 | |
| Bank Charges | 75.00 | |
| Computer Supplies | 5,885.00 | |
| Office Expenses | 3,247.00 | |
| Rent or Lease | 265.00 | |
| Repair & Maintenance | 215.00 | |
| Utilities | 606.00 | |
| TOTAL | $24,825.00 | $24,825.00 |

## October 1 through December 31, 20XX Income Statement

**XXXXXXX Service Corporation**
**Profit & Loss**
October - December, 2003

| | Total |
|---|---|
| **Income** | |
| Services | 16,625.00 |
| Total Income | $16,625.00 |
| **Expenses** | |
| Advertising | 270.00 |
| Bank Charges | 75.00 |
| Computer Supplies | 5,885.00 |
| Office Expenses | 3,247.00 |
| Rent or Lease | 265.00 |
| Repair and Maintenance | 215.00 |
| Utilities | 606.00 |
| Total Expenses | $10,563.00 |
| Net Operating Income | $6,062.00 |
| Net Income | $6,062.00 |

## December's Balance Sheet

**XXXXXXX Service Corporation**
**Balance Sheet**
As of December 31, 2003

|  | Total |
|---|---|
| **ASSETS** | |
| **Current Assets** | |
| **Bank Accounts** | |
| XXXXXXX  Service Corporation | 5,852.00 |
| **Total Bank Accounts** | $5,852.00 |
| **Accounts Receivable** | |
| Accounts Receivable | 0.00 |
| **Total Accounts Receivable** | $0.00 |
| **Other Current Assets** | |
| Prepaid Insurance | 410.00 |
| **Total Other Current Assets** | $410.00 |
| **Total Current Assets** | $6,262.00 |
| **Fixed Assets** | |
| **Computer Equipment** | |
| Accumulated Depreciation | -1,200.00 |
| Original Cost | 6,000.00 |
| **Total Computer Equipment** | $4,800.00 |
| **Total Fixed Assets** | $4,800.00 |
| **TOTAL ASSETS** | $11,062.00 |
| **LIABILITIES AND EQUITY** | |
| **Liabilities** | |
| **Current Liabilities** | |
| **Accounts Payable** | |
| Accounts Payable | 0.00 |
| **Total Accounts Payable** | $0.00 |
| **Total Current Liabilities** | $0.00 |
| **Total Liabilities** | $0.00 |
| **Equity** | |
| Common Stock | 1,000.00 |
| Dividends | -2,000.00 |
| Paid in Capital | 6,000.00 |
| Retained Earnings | |
| Net Income | 6,062.00 |
| **Total Equity** | $11,062.00 |
| **TOTAL LIABILITIES AND EQUITY** | $11,062.00 |

## CHECK YOUR PROGRESS

### Internet Homework

If necessary, start QuickBooks: Online Edition, and then log in to your account.

1. On the QuickBooks: Online Edition home page under <u>Subscription Information</u> click on <u>What happens after my trial?</u>

2. Read to learn about the three actions you can take you're your trial period expires.

3. When you are finished reading the information in the box, return to the home page screen by closing the box.

4. Link to <u>Privacy and Security</u> and read to learn more about these important issues.

5. Write a summary of what your learned about what QuickBooks: Online Edition is doing about privacy and security. The minimum length of each essay should be 25 words; the maximum length 75 words.

6. Use a word-processing program to type your reports.

**Multiple-Choice.**  In the space provided, write the letter that best answers each question.

_____1.    Fourth quarter transactions are for the months of:

   a.  January, February, and March.
   b.  April, May, and June.
   c.  July, August, and September.
   d.  October, November, and December.
   e.  None of the above.

_____2.    The Accounting Essentials web site is located at:

   a.  www.mhhe.com/yachtessentials2e
   b.  www.QuickBooks:  Online Edition.com
   c.  www.google.com
   d.  www.QuickBooks:  Online Editionsupport.com
   e.  None of the above.

_____3.    Which QuickBooks:  Online Edition menu bar areas do you access to complete fourth-quarter record keeping?

   a.  Banking.
   b.  Customers.
   c.  Vendors.
   d.  Report.
   e.  All of the above.

_____4.    Another word used for supplier is:

   a.  Vendor.
   b.  Customer.
   c.  Sales discount.
   d.  Inventory.
   e.  All of the above.

_____5.   Which of the following is the name of one of your vendors?

    a.   Two Sisters B & B
    b.   Connections Cafe
    c.   Big Bytes Supplies
    d.   Charity Access
    e.   None of the above.

_____6.   Which of the following is the name of one of your customers?

    a.   Two Sisters B & B
    b.   Sales Products Supply
    c.   Big Bytes Supplies
    d.   Student name.
    e.   None of the above.

_____7.   To record purchases of supplies from vendors, you use which of the following links?

    a.   Enter invoices.
    b.   Pay sales tax.
    c.   Enter bills.
    d.   Make vendor payment.
    e.   None of the above.

_____8.   To return supplies purchased from a vendor, you use which of the following links?

    a.   Return supplies.
    b.   Enter credits.
    c.   Enter vendor credits.
    d.   Pay bills.
    e.   None of the above.

Text and screen variations may occur since web-based software products backup and upgrade automatically.

_____9.    What report would you display or print to see the balance in your accounts payable account?

    a.  A/R Register.
    b.  A/P Register.
    c.  Income Statement.
    d.  Reconciliation Summary.
    e.  None of the above.

_____10.    What report would you display or print to see the balance in your accounts receivable account?

    a.  A/R Register.
    b.  A/P Register.
    c.  Income Statement.
    d.  Reconciliation Summary.
    e.  None of the above.

**True/False.** Write T for True and F for false in the space provided.

_____11.   When your business makes purchases on account from vendors, the transactions are known as accounts receivable transactions.

_____12.   When your business makes sales on account to customers, these transactions are knows as accounts payable transactions.

_____13.   Entering bills as soon as you receive them, keeps your cash flow reports up to date.

_____14.   You can use the "Pay Bills" link and the "Pay One Vendor" link to pay amounts owed to vendors.

_____15.   The "Items List" link under "Customers" on the QuickBooks: Online Edition menu bar allows you to access the prices of your services.

_____16.   To record customer transactions, you use the "Create Invoices" link.

_____17.   To edit customer information, you use the "Customer List."

_____18.   To write checks, you link to "Write Checks" under "Company" on the QuickBooks:  Online Edition menu bar.

_____19.   If a customer returns supplies to you, you use the "Give Refund or Credit" link to record this return.

_____20.   Once you issue an invoice to a customer, that customer owes your business money.

**Exercise 4-1.** Using the reports that you printed for December, answer the following questions.

1.  Your business' Net Income at the end of the
    fourth quarter is:                                    _____

5.  On December 31, 20XX, your prepaid insurance
    account shows the following balance:                 _____

3.  On December 31, 20XX, your accounts receivable
    account shows the following balance:                 _____

4.  On December 31, 20XX, your checking account
    shows the following balance:                         _____

5.  On December 31, 20XX, your accounts payable
    account shows the following balance:                 _____

**Exercise 4-2.** Copy your December 31, 20XX balance sheet to Excel. Use **Your Name** and **Exercise 4-2** as the file name. Print your Excel balance sheet.

## PART 4 INDEX

# 5 End-of-Year & Beginning-of-Year Transactions

In Part 5 of *Computer Accounting Essentials Using QuickBooks: Online Edition*, you will complete end-of-year adjusting entries and print financial statements. Part 5 also includes transactions for the start of the new year –January 1 - 31, 20XX.

**SOFTWARE OBJECTIVES: In Part 5, you use the software to:**

1. Record end-of-year adjusting entries.
2. Print the adjusted trial balance and end-of-quarter reports.
3. Record end-of-year closing entries.
4. Print the post-closing trial balance.
5. Close the accounting period.
6. Complete January 1 - 31, 20XX transactions.
7. Copy data to Excel.
8. Complete activities for Part 5, End-of-Year & Beginning-of-Year transactions.

**WEB OBJECTIVES: In Part 5, you use the Internet to:**

1. Access the Computer Accounting Essentials web site at www.mhhe.com/yachtessentials2e to check for updates.
2. Log in to your QuickBooks: Online Edition account.
3. Record end-of-year and beginning-of-year transactions.
4. Complete Internet activities.

**COMPUTER ACCOUNTING ESSENTIALS WEB SITE**

Before you begin your work in Part 5, End-of-Year and Beginning-of-Year Transactions, access the Computer Accounting Essentials web site at www.mhhe.com/yachtessentials2e. Software and book updates will be shown. Check this web site regularly for reference and study.

## GETTING STARTED

Follow these steps to start QuickBooks: Online Edition. You *must* complete Parts 1, 2, 3, and 4, pages 3 – 141, before starting Part 5, End-of-Year & Beginning-of-Year Transactions. *The exercises at the end of each part must be completed, too.*

1. Start your Internet browser and log in to QuickBooks: Online Edition in the usual way.

2. Move your mouse over "Banking" on the QuickBooks: Online Edition menu bar. When the drop-down menu appears, click on <u>Make Journal Entry</u>.

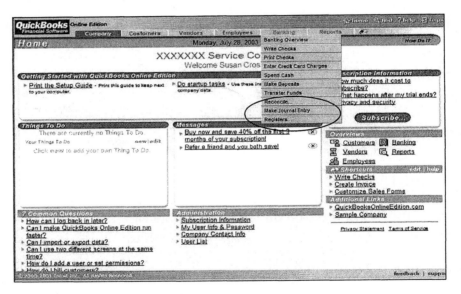

The "Make Journal Entry" screen appears.

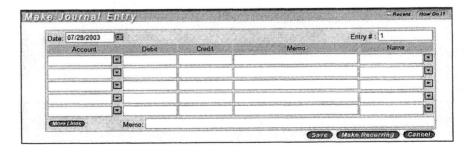

---

Text and screen variations may occur since web-based software products backup and upgrade automatically.

## END-OF-YEAR ADJUSTING ENTRIES

The **general journal** shows the debits and credits of transactions, and can be used to record any type of transaction.  For purposes of this exercise, you will use the general journal to record adjusting entries.

In Parts 4 of *Computer Accounting Essentials Using QuickBooks:  Online Edition,* you used selections from the "Customers," "Vendors," and "Banking" drop-down menus to record business transactions.  For adjusting entries, you will use the Make Journal Entry link from the "Banking" list, which takes you to QuickBooks:  Online Edition's "Make Journal Entry" screen.  Compare your screen to the one shown on page 144.

---

**Comment:**
Journal entries are in debit/credit format and must always be in balance. QuickBooks:  Online Edition will show you any out-of-balance amount at the top of the "Make Journal Entry" screen and will *not* let you submit the entry until it is balanced.

---

Follow these steps to record adjusting entries in the general journal for December 31, 20XX:

1.  The "Make Journal Entry" window should be displayed on your screen.  Change the date to December 31, 20XX.

2.  Type **Adjust 1** in the "Entry No." field.  (For the subsequent adjusting entry, type **Adjust 2**.)

3.  In the "Account" field, select or type the appropriate account to debit.

4.  In the "Debit" amount field, type the appropriate amount.

5.  In the next  "Account" field, select or type the appropriate account to credit.

6.  When you click on the "Credit" field, the amount is automatically completed or you can type in the appropriate amount.

7.  Type any memo information, optional.

---

8. Click on "Save."

9. In a few moments, a new "Make Journal Entry" screen will appear to record the next entry.

Record the following adjusting entries for December 31, 20XX:

1. Adjust 1:  Use straight-line depreciation for the business' equipment. The equipment has a five-year service life and no salvage value.  To depreciate the equipment for the year, use this calculation:  $6,000/5 years = $1,200.00.  (*Hint: For Account:  First line-- scroll to bottom of the pull-down menu and select "Depreciation Expense—Other Expense."   For second line—from the pull-down menu select "Computer Equipment—Accumulated Depreciation—Fixed Assets."*)

| Account Name | Debit | Credit |
|---|---|---|
| Depreciation Expense – Other Expense | 1,200.00 | |
| Computer Equipment - Accumulated Depreciation—Fixed Assets | | 1,200.00 |

Compare your screen to the following then click on <u>Save</u>.

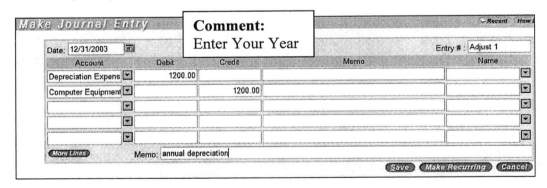

2. Adjust 2:  During the year, $200 of Prepaid insurance expired.

| Account Name | Debit | Credit |
|---|---|---|
| Insurance - Expense | 200.00 | |
| Prepaid Insurance – Other Current Asset | | 200.00 |

Compare your screen to the following then click on <u>Save</u>.

---

Text and screen variations may occur since web-based software products backup and upgrade automatically.

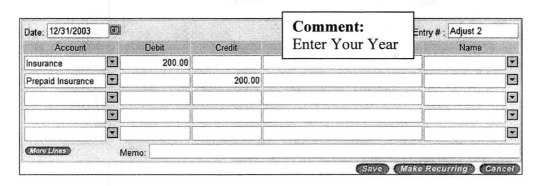

3. Display or print the "Transaction List with Splits" report for December 31, 20XX. Compare with the one shown below.

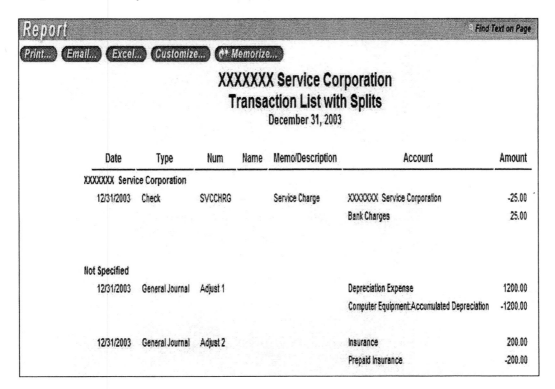

Observe that the first entry for December 31 is the bank service charge. Adjustments 1 and 2 are shown after the service charge.

## PRINTING THE ADJUSTED TRIAL BALANCE

Print the trial balance and compare with the one shown below.

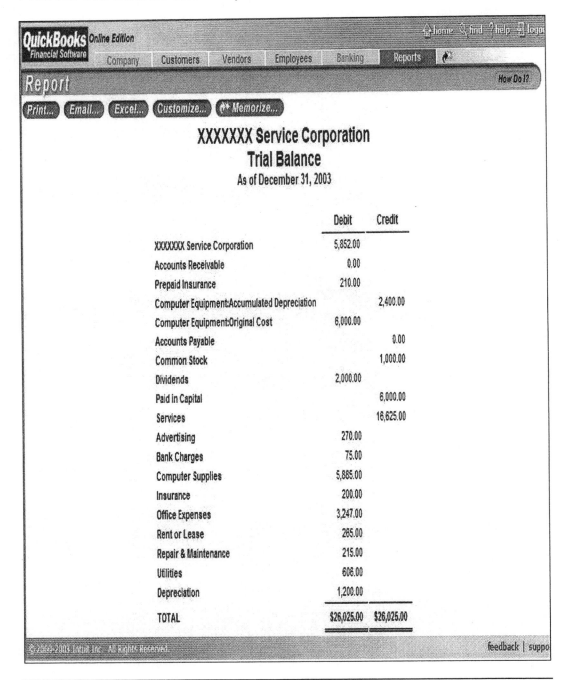

**XXXXXX Service Corporation**
**Trial Balance**
As of December 31, 2003

| | Debit | Credit |
|---|---|---|
| XXXXXX Service Corporation | 5,852.00 | |
| Accounts Receivable | 0.00 | |
| Prepaid Insurance | 210.00 | |
| Computer Equipment:Accumulated Depreciation | | 2,400.00 |
| Computer Equipment:Original Cost | 6,000.00 | |
| Accounts Payable | | 0.00 |
| Common Stock | | 1,000.00 |
| Dividends | 2,000.00 | |
| Paid in Capital | | 6,000.00 |
| Services | | 16,625.00 |
| Advertising | 270.00 | |
| Bank Charges | 75.00 | |
| Computer Supplies | 5,885.00 | |
| Insurance | 200.00 | |
| Office Expenses | 3,247.00 | |
| Rent or Lease | 265.00 | |
| Repair & Maintenance | 215.00 | |
| Utilities | 606.00 | |
| Depreciation | 1,200.00 | |
| TOTAL | $26,025.00 | $26,025.00 |

Text and screen variations may occur since web-based software products backup and upgrade automatically.

## PRINTING END-OF-YEAR FINANCIAL STATEMENTS

1. Print the Income Statement from 10/1/20XX to 12/31/0X.  Compare your printout with the one shown below.

**Income Statement**

### XXXXXXX Service Corporation
### Profit & Loss
January - December 2003

|  | Total |
|---|---|
| **Income** | |
| Services | 16,625.00 |
| **Total Income** | **$16,625.00** |
| **Expenses** | |
| Advertising | 270.00 |
| Bank Charges | 75.00 |
| Computer Supplies | 5,885.00 |
| Insurance | 200.00 |
| Office Expenses | 3,247.00 |
| Rent or Lease | 265.00 |
| Repair & Maintenance | 215.00 |
| Utilities | 606.00 |
| **Total Expenses** | **$10,763.00** |
| **Net Operating Income** | **$5,862.00** |
| **Other Expenses** | |
| Depreciation | 1,200.00 |
| **Total Other Expenses** | **$1,200.00** |
| **Net Other Income** | **$ -1,200.00** |
| **Net Income** | **$4,662.00** |

2. Print the balance sheet and compare with the one shown on next page.

**Balance Sheet**

## XXXXXXX Service Corporation
## Balance Sheet
### As of December 31, 2003

|  | Total |
|---|---|
| **ASSETS** | |
| Current Assets | |
| Bank Accounts | |
| XXXXXXX Service Corporation | 5,852.00 |
| Total Bank Accounts | $5,852.00 |
| Accounts Receivable | |
| Accounts Receivable | 0.00 |
| Total Accounts Receivable | $0.00 |
| Other Current Assets | |
| Prepaid Insurance | 210.00 |
| Total Other Current Assets | $210.00 |
| Total Current Assets | $6,062.00 |
| Fixed Assets | |
| Computer Equipment | |
| Accumulated Depreciation | -2,400.00 |
| Original Cost | 6,000.00 |
| Total Computer Equipment | $3,600.00 |
| Total Fixed Assets | $3,600.00 |
| TOTAL ASSETS | $9,662.00 |
| **LIABILITIES AND EQUITY** | |
| Liabilities | |
| Current Liabilities | |
| Accounts Payable | |
| Accounts Payable | 0.00 |
| Total Accounts Payable | $0.00 |
| Total Current Liabilities | $0.00 |
| Total Liabilities | $0.00 |
| Equity | |
| Common Stock | 1,000.00 |
| Dividends | -2,000.00 |
| Paid in Capital | 6,000.00 |
| Retained Earnings | |
| Net Income | 4,662.00 |
| Total Equity | $9,662.00 |
| TOTAL LIABILITIES AND EQUITY | $9,662.00 |

Text and screen variations may occur since web-based software products backup and upgrade automatically.

## END-OF-YEAR CLOSING ENTRIES

As you know from your study of accounting, the purpose of *closing entries* is to reset revenue, expense, and dividends account balances to zero. When you record and post closing entries, you are transferring the end-of-year (or end-of-period) balances in revenue, expense, and dividends accounts to the retained earnings account.

The adjusted trial balance (page 148) and end-of-quarter Income Statement (page 149) were used to determine the closing entries. Click on "Save" between each entry to post. Record the closing entries in the **general journal** *(Hint: Use the* Make Journal Entry *link from the* "Banking" *list).*

1. Close 1: Close revenue accounts. *(Hint: After typing "Income Summary" in the account field, a "Mini Interview will appear to guide you through the process of adding this new account. The answers to the mini interview include: "Choose from all account types" for the account type, "equity" for detail type of expense, "accumulated adjustment" for the type of equity, and "Income Summary" for the name of the account. Leave the description and balance information blank.)*

| Date | Account Name | Debit | Credit |
|---|---|---|---|
| 12/31/20XX | Services-Income | 16,625.00 | |
| | Income Summary | | 16,625.00 |

2. Close 2: Close expense accounts.

| Date | Account Name | Debit | Credit |
|---|---|---|---|
| 12/31/20XX | Income Summary | 11,963.00 | |
| | Advertising | | 270.00 |
| | Bank Service Charges | | 75.00 |
| | Computer Supplies | | 5,885.00 |
| | Depreciation | | 1,200.00 |
| | Insurance Expense | | 200.00 |
| | Office Expenses | | 3,247.00 |
| | Rent or Lease | | 265.00 |
| | Repairs & Maintenance | | 215.00 |
| | Utilities | | 606.00 |

3. Close 3: Close Income Summary account.

| Date | Account Name | Debit | Credit |
|---|---|---|---|
| 12/31/20XX | Income Summary | 4,662.00 | |
| | Retained Earnings | | 4,662.00 |

4. Close 4: Close Dividends account.

| Date | Account Name | Debit | Credit |
|---|---|---|---|
| 12/31/20XX | Retained Earnings | 2,000.00 | |
| | Dividends | | 2,000.00 |

## TRANSACTION LIST BY DAY REPORT

To make sure that you have entered all the closing entries, you should display your "Transaction List with Splits" report and compare it with the one shown below. This report will show all your December 31 entries: bank service charges, adjusting entries, and closing entries.

### December 31, 20XX Transaction List

**XXXXXXX Service Corporation**
**Transaction List with Splits**
December 31, 2003

| Date | Type | Num | Name | Memo/Description | Account | Amount |
|---|---|---|---|---|---|---|
| **XXXXXXX Service Corporation** | | | | | | |
| 12/31/2003 | Check | SVCCHRG | | Service Charge | XXXXXXX Service Corporation | -25.00 |
| | | | | | Bank Charges | 25.00 |
| **Not Specified** | | | | | | |
| 12/31/2003 | General Journal | Adjust 1 | | | Depreciation Expense | 1200.00 |
| | | | | | Computer Equipment:Accumulated Depreciation | -1200.00 |
| 12/31/2003 | General Journal | Adjust 2 | | | Insurance | 200.00 |
| | | | | | Prepaid Insurance | -200.00 |
| 12/31/2003 | General Journal | Close 1 | | | Services | -18625.00 |
| | | | | | Income Summary | 18625.00 |
| 12/31/2003 | General Journal | Close 2 | | | Income Summary | -11963.00 |
| | | | | | Advertising | -270.00 |
| | | | | | Bank Charges | -75.00 |
| | | | | | Computer Supplies | -5685.00 |
| | | | | | Depreciation Expense | -1200.00 |
| | | | | | Insurance | -200.00 |
| | | | | | Office Expenses | -3247.00 |
| | | | | | Rent or Lease | -265.00 |
| | | | | | Repair and Maintenance | -215.00 |
| | | | | | Utilities | -806.00 |
| 12/31/2003 | General Journal | Close 3 | | | Income Summary | -4662.00 |
| | | | | | Retained Earnings | 4662.00 |
| 12/31/2003 | General Journal | Close 4 | | | Retained Earnings | -2000.00 |
| | | | | | Dividends | 2000.00 |

Text and screen variations may occur since web-based software products backup and upgrade automatically.

## POST-CLOSING TRIAL BALANCE

Make the appropriate selections to print a trial balance for December 31, 20XX. You may want to compare your post-closing trial balance to the one below:

### XXXXXXX Service Corporation
### Trial Balance
As of December 31, 2003

| | Debit | Credit |
|---|---|---|
| XXXXXXX Service Corporation | 5,852.00 | |
| Accounts Receivable | 0.00 | |
| Prepaid Insurance | 210.00 | |
| Computer Equipment:Accumulated Depreciation | | 2,400.00 |
| Computer Equipment:Original Cost | 6,000.00 | |
| Accounts Payable | | 0.00 |
| Common Stock | | 1,000.00 |
| Dividends | | 0.00 |
| Income Summary | | 0.00 |
| Paid in Capital | | 6,000.00 |
| Retained Earnings | | 2,662.00 |
| Services | | 0.00 |
| Advertising | 0.00 | |
| Bank Charges | 0.00 | |
| Computer Supplies | 0.00 | |
| Insurance | 0.00 | |
| Office Expenses | 0.00 | |
| Rent or Lease | 0.00 | |
| Repair & Maintenance | 0.00 | |
| Utilities | 0.00 | |
| Depreciation | 0.00 | |
| TOTAL | $12,062.00 | $12,062.00 |

Observe that your dividends, income, and expense accounts all have zero balances. Also, your Retained Earnings account now has a balance $2,662.00.

## BEGINNING-OF-YEAR TRANSACTIONS

Before you start entering transactions for January 20XX, let's look at the balance sheet. Make the appropriate entries to print your balance sheet for January 1, 20XX. (*Hint: Remember to use the next year in your date. For example, if you have been using December 2004, you will now use January 2005.*) Compare your printout with the one shown below.

**XXXXXXX Service Corporation**
**Balance Sheet**
As of January 1, 2004

| Comment |
|---|
| Your new year, i.e., 2005 or 2006 |

|  | Total |
|---|---|
| **ASSETS** | |
| Current Assets | |
| Bank Accounts | |
| XXXXXXX Service Corporation | 5,852.00 |
| Total Bank Accounts | $5,852.00 |
| Accounts Receivable | |
| Accounts Receivable | 0.00 |
| Total Accounts Receivable | $0.00 |
| Other Current Assets | |
| Prepaid Insurance | 210.00 |
| Total Other Current Assets | $210.00 |
| Total Current Assets | $6,062.00 |
| Fixed Assets | |
| Computer Equipment | |
| Accumulated Depreciation | -2,400.00 |
| Original Cost | 6,000.00 |
| Total Computer Equipment | $3,600.00 |
| Total Fixed Assets | $3,600.00 |
| TOTAL ASSETS | $9,662.00 |
| **LIABILITIES AND EQUITY** | |
| Liabilities | |
| Current Liabilities | |
| Accounts Payable | |
| Accounts Payable | 0.00 |
| Total Accounts Payable | $0.00 |
| Total Current Liabilities | $0.00 |
| Total Liabilities | $0.00 |
| Equity | |
| Common Stock | 1,000.00 |
| Dividends | 0.00 |
| Income Summary | 0.00 |
| Paid in Capital | 6,000.00 |
| Retained Earnings | 2,662.00 |
| Net Income | 0.00 |
| Total Equity | $9,662.00 |
| TOTAL LIABILITIES AND EQUITY | $9,662.00 |

Text and screen variations may occur since web-based software products backup and upgrade automatically.

| Date | Transaction |
|---|---|
| 1/02/20XX | Issued hand-written Check No. 25 to Santa Fe Rentals for equipment rental, $192. |
| 1/02/20XX | Received Invoice 135JE and shipment from Big Bytes Supplies for the purchase of computer supplies on credit, Net 30, $1,775. |
| 1/03/20XX | Received Invoice EX99 and shipment from Sales Products Supply for the purchase of office supplies on credit, Net 30, $175. |
| 1/08/20XX | Sold 50 hours of maintenance services on account to Two Sisters B & B, Invoice Net 30, $1,500. |
| 1/08/20XX | Sold  2 hours of maintenance services, 10 hours of repair services, and 10 hours of new service on account to Connections Cafe, Invoice Net 30, $1,560. |
| 1/08/20XX | Returned to Big Bytes Supplies computer supplies, Invoice 135JE, for vendor credit, $100. |
| 1/11/20XX | Paid Big Bytes Supplies, Invoice 135JE, for the January 2 purchase less January 8 return, hand-written Check No. 26, $1,675. |
| 1/11/20XX | Paid Sales Products Supply, Invoice EX99, for the January 3 purchase, hand-written Check No. 27, $175. |
| 1/17/20XX | Received a check from Connections Cafe in payment of Invoice, Check No. 5510, $1,560. |
| 1/17/20XX | Received a check from Two Sisters B & B in payment of Invoice, Check No. 335, $1,500. |
| 1/24/20XX | Cash sales $680, received check No. 804 for 10 hours of repair services and 6 hours of maintenance services. |
| 1/30/20XX | Issued Check No. 28 to Comtel for monthly telephone and Internet service, $279. |

✓1/30/20XX     Issued Check No. 29 to Regional Utilities for monthly utilities bill, $201.

✓1/30/20XX     Issued Check No. 30 for payment of dividends $2,000 from checking account.

## RECONCILE THE BANK STATEMENT: JANUARY

The business receives a bank statement every month for your regular checking account. The bank statement shows that checks and deposits have cleared the bank. Use the bank statement below to complete account reconciliation for January.

| REGULAR CHECKING ACCOUNT January 1 - 31, 20XX | | | |
|---|---|---|---|
| Previous Balance | | $6,630.00 | |
| 3 Deposits (+) | | 3,740.00 | |
| 7 Checks (-) | | 2,820.00 | |
| Service Charges (-) | 1/31/XX | 25.00 | |
| **Ending Balance** | 1/31/XX | **$7,525.00** | |
| DEPOSITS | | | |
| | 1/19 | 1,560.00 | |
| | 1/19 | 1,500.00 | |
| | 1/25 | 680.00 | |
| CHECKS (Asterisk * indicates break in check number sequence) | | | |
| 1/5 | 21 | 303.00 | |
| 1/5 | 22 | 190.00 | |
| 1/5 | 23 | 145.00 | |
| 1/5 | 24 | 140.00 | |
| 1/5 | 25 | 192.00 | |
| 1/13 | 26 | 1,675.00 | |
| 1/13 | 27 | 175.00 | |

From the "Banking" drop-down menu, go to the link for <u>Reconcile</u>. Complete the steps for reconciling your January bank statement. Then, compare your Reconciliation Summary to the one shown on the next page.

**Comment:**
If a check or deposit does *not* appear on your "Reconcile" screen, move your mouse over the QuickBooks: Online Edition menu bar to access the appropriate drop-down menu. Then, select the appropriate link. Select the "Edit" button and make any needed corrections. To update the record, click on "Save."

Text and screen variations may occur since web-based software products backup and upgrade automatically.

## January's Reconciliation Summary

**XXXXXXX Service Corporation**
**Reconcile Report for XXXXXXX Service Corporation**
This is a static report. Any changes to transactions since the reconcile date are not reflected here.
Report created on 07/28/2003.

Account: XXXXXX Service Corporation
Statement Date: 01/31/2004
Reconcile Date: 07/28/2003

**Summary**

| | |
|---|---|
| Opening Balance | 6630.00 |
| Ending Balance of Statement | 7525.00 |
| Uncleared Amount | -2480.00 |
| Register Balance as of Reconcile Date | 5045.00 |

**Cleared Transactions**

| Date | Type | Num | Payee | Amount |
|---|---|---|---|---|
| **Cleared Checks and Payments** | | | | |
| 12/30/2003 | Check | 21 | Comtel | 303.00 |
| 12/30/2003 | Check | 22 | Regional Utilities | 190.00 |
| 12/30/2003 | Check | 23 | Sun News | 145.00 |
| 12/30/2003 | Check | 24 | Jonathan Brent | 140.00 |
| 01/02/2004 | Check | 25 | Santa Fe Rentals | 192.00 |
| 01/11/2004 | Bill Pmt | 26 | Big Bytes Supplies | 1675.00 |
| 01/11/2004 | Bill Pmt | 27 | Sales Products Supply | 175.00 |
| 01/31/2004 | Check | SVCCHRG | | 25.00 |
| | | | | Subtotal: 2845.00 |
| **Cleared Deposits and Other Credits** | | | | |
| 01/17/2004 | Payment | 5510 | Connections Cafe | 1560.00 |
| 01/17/2004 | Payment | 335 | Two Sisters B&B | 1500.00 |
| 01/24/2004 | Sales Receipt | 804 | Cash Sales | 680.00 |
| | | | | Subtotal: 3740.00 |
| **Total Cleared Transactions** | | | | 895.00 |

**Uncleared Transactions as of 01/31/2004**

| Date | Type | Num | Payee | Amount |
|---|---|---|---|---|
| **Uncleared Checks and Payments** | | | | |
| 01/30/2004 | Check | 28 | Comtel | 279.00 |
| 01/30/2004 | Check | 29 | Regional Utilities | 201.00 |
| 01/30/2004 | Check | 30 | XXXXXXX | 2000.00 |
| | | | | Subtotal: 2480.00 |
| **Uncleared Deposits and Other Credits** | | | | |
| | | | | Subtotal: 0.00 |

**PRINTING JANUARY REPORTS**

Print the following reports and compare them to the ones shown on pages 159 - 161.

1.  Print the "Transaction List by Day" report for January 1, 20XX through January 31, 20XX.  Compare your report to the one shown on page 159.

2.  Print the January 31, 20XX trial balance.  Compare your report to the one shown on page 160.  (If you set your printer to landscape for the transaction detail report, remember to set it back to portrait for the trial balance.)

3.  Print the January 1, 20XX through January 31, 20XX income statement.  Compare your report to the one shown on page 160.

4.  Print the January 31, 20XX balance sheet.  Compare your report to the one shown on page 161.

## January's Transaction List

**Comment**
Your new year,
i.e., 2005 or 2006

### XXXXXXX Service Corporation
### Transaction List by Day
January 2004

| Date | Type | Num | Name | Account | Split | Amount |
|------|------|-----|------|---------|-------|--------|
| **January 2, 2004** | | | | | | |
| 01/02/2004 | Check | 25 | Santa Fe Rentals | XXXXXXX Service Corporation | Rent or Lease | -192.00 |
| 01/02/2004 | Bill | 135JE | Big Bytes Supplies | Accounts Payable | Computer Supplies | 1775.00 |
| Total for January 2, 2004 | | | | | | $1,583.00 |
| **January 3, 2004** | | | | | | |
| 01/03/2004 | Bill | EX99 | Sales Products Supply | Accounts Payable | Office Expenses | 175.00 |
| Total for January 3, 2004 | | | | | | $175.00 |
| **January 8, 2004** | | | | | | |
| 01/08/2004 | Invoice | 1018 | Two Sisters B&B | Accounts Receivable | Services | 1500.00 |
| 01/08/2004 | Invoice | 1019 | Connections Cafe | Accounts Receivable | -SPLIT- | 1560.00 |
| 01/08/2004 | Vendor Credit | 135JE | Big Bytes Supplies | Accounts Payable | Computer Supplies | -100.00 |
| Total for January 8, 2004 | | | | | | $2,960.00 |
| **January 11, 2004** | | | | | | |
| 01/11/2004 | Bill Payment (Check) | 26 | Big Bytes Supplies | XXXXXXX Service Corporation | -SPLIT- | -1675.00 |
| 01/11/2004 | Bill Payment (Check) | 27 | Sales Products Supply | XXXXXXX Service Corporation | Accounts Payable | -175.00 |
| Total for January 11, 2004 | | | | | | $ -1,850.00 |
| **January 17, 2004** | | | | | | |
| 01/17/2004 | Payment | 5510 | Connections Cafe | XXXXXXX Service Corporation | Accounts Receivable | 1560.00 |
| 01/17/2004 | Payment | 335 | Two Sisters B&B | XXXXXXX Service Corporation | Accounts Receivable | 1500.00 |
| Total for January 17, 2004 | | | | | | $3,060.00 |
| **January 24, 2004** | | | | | | |
| 01/24/2004 | Sales Receipt | 1020 | Cash Sales | XXXXXXX Service Corporation | -SPLIT- | 680.00 |
| Total for January 24, 2004 | | | | | | $680.00 |
| **January 30, 2004** | | | | | | |
| 01/30/2004 | Check | 28 | Comtel | XXXXXXX Service Corporation | Office Expenses | -279.00 |
| 01/30/2004 | Check | 29 | Regional Utilities | XXXXXXX Service Corporation | Utilities | -201.00 |
| 01/30/2004 | Check | 30 | Susan Crosson | XXXXXXX Service Corporation | Dividends | -2000.00 |
| Total for January 30, 2004 | | | | | | $ -2,480.00 |
| **January 31, 2004** | | | | | | |
| 01/31/2004 | Check | SVCCHRG | | XXXXXXX Service Corporation | Bank Charges | -25.00 |
| Total for January 31, 2004 | | | | | | $ -25.00 |

## January's Trial Balance

**XXXXXXX Service Corporation**
**Trial Balance**
As of January 31, 2004

| | Debit | Credit |
|---|---|---|
| XXXXXXX Service Corporation | 5,045.00 | |
| Accounts Receivable | 0.00 | |
| Prepaid Insurance | 210.00 | |
| Computer Equipment:Accumulated Depreciation | | 2,400.00 |
| Computer Equipment:Original Cost | 6,000.00 | |
| Accounts Payable | | 0.00 |
| Common Stock | | 1,000.00 |
| Dividends | 2,000.00 | |
| Income Summary | | 0.00 |
| Paid in Capital | | 6,000.00 |
| Retained Earnings | | 2,662.00 |
| Services | | 3,740.00 |
| Advertising | 0.00 | |
| Bank Charges | 25.00 | |
| Computer Supplies | 1,675.00 | |
| Insurance | 0.00 | |
| Office Expenses | 454.00 | |
| Rent or Lease | 192.00 | |
| Repair & Maintenance | 0.00 | |
| Utilities | 201.00 | |
| Depreciation | 0.00 | |
| TOTAL | $15,802.00 | $15,802.00 |

> **Comment**
> Your new year,
> i.e., 2005 or 2006

## January's Income Statement

**XXXXXXX Service Corporation**
**Profit & Loss**
January 2004

| | Total |
|---|---|
| **Income** | |
| Services | 3,740.00 |
| **Total Income** | $3,740.00 |
| **Expenses** | |
| Bank Charges | 25.00 |
| Computer Supplies | 1,675.00 |
| Office Expenses | 454.00 |
| Rent or Lease | 192.00 |
| Utilities | 201.00 |
| **Total Expenses** | $2,547.00 |
| **Net Operating Income** | $1,193.00 |
| **Net Income** | $1,193.00 |

> **Comment**
> Your new year,
> i.e., 2005 or 2006

Text and screen variations may occur since web-based software products backup and upgrade automatically.

## January's Balance Sheet

**XXXXXXX Service Corporation**
**Balance Sheet**
As of January 31, 2004

| | Total |
|---|---|
| ASSETS | |
| Current Assets | |
| Bank Accounts | |
| XXXXXXX Service Corporation | 5,045.00 |
| Total Bank Accounts | $5,045.00 |
| Accounts Receivable | |
| Accounts Receivable | 0.00 |
| Total Accounts Receivable | $0.00 |
| Other Current Assets | |
| Prepaid Insurance | 210.00 |
| Total Other Current Assets | $210.00 |
| Total Current Assets | $5,255.00 |
| Fixed Assets | |
| Computer Equipment | |
| Accumulated Depreciation | -2,400.00 |
| Original Cost | 6,000.00 |
| Total Computer Equipment | $3,600.00 |
| Total Fixed Assets | $3,600.00 |
| TOTAL ASSETS | $8,855.00 |
| LIABILITIES AND EQUITY | |
| Liabilities | |
| Current Liabilities | |
| Accounts Payable | |
| Accounts Payable | 0.00 |
| Total Accounts Payable | $0.00 |
| Total Current Liabilities | $0.00 |
| Total Liabilities | $0.00 |
| Equity | |
| Common Stock | 1,000.00 |
| Dividends | -2,000.00 |
| Income Summary | 0.00 |
| Paid in Capital | 6,000.00 |
| Retained Earnings | 2,662.00 |
| Net Income | 1,193.00 |
| Total Equity | $8,855.00 |
| TOTAL LIABILITIES AND EQUITY | $8,855.00 |

> **Comment**
> Your new year,
> i.e., 2005 or 2006

## CHECK YOUR PROGRESS

### Internet Homework

If necessary, start QuickBooks: Online Edition, and then log in to your account. Using selections from your QuickBooks: Online Edition account, answer the following questions. Answer each question in the space provided.

1. List ways you can get QuickBooks: Online Edition to run faster. (*Hint: Click on the* Can I make QuickBooks: Online Edition run faster? *link under "Common Questions" on your company's home page.*)

   _____

   _____

   _____

   _____

2. If you want to accept credit card payments, what does that feature cost? (*Hint: Click on the appropriate link on the QuickBooksOnline Edition.com website*)

   _____

   _____

   _____

   _____

Text and screen variations may occur since web-based software products backup and upgrade automatically.

3.  Briefly describe two other products offered by QuickBooks.  (*Hint: Click on the "Additional links.").*

    _____

    _____

    _____

    _____

4.  Click on ▨ help on the QuickBooks:  Online Edition menu bar. Explain various ways to use this feature.

    _____

    _____

    _____

    _____

    _____

**Multiple-Choice.** In the space provided, write the letter that best answers each question.

_____1.    In Part 5, the general journal is used to record which of the following transactions?

   a. Purchases.
   b. Sales.
   c. Adjusting entries.
   d. Credit memos for customers.
   e. None of the above.

_____2.    Adjusting entries are dated:

   a. The first day of the month.
   b. The last day of the month.
   c.  Any day of the month.
   d. All of the above.
   e. None of the above.

_____3.    To depreciate your business's fixed assets, you used which one of the following deprecation methods?

   a. Sum-of-the-years digits.
   b. Units of production.
   c. MACRS.
   d. Straight-line.
   e. None of the above.

_____4.    The amount of the adjusting entry for depreciation expense-- equipment was:

   a. $5,000.00.
   b. $1,200.00.
   c. $2,333.33.
   d. $1,000.00.
   e. None of the above.

_____5.    The amount of the adjusting entry for expired insurance was:

a. $200.00.
b. $410.00.
c. $210.00.
d. $1,200.00.
e. None of the above.

_____6.    The total debit and credit balance on your adjusted trial balance is:

a. $26,025.00.
b.  $4,658.00.
c. $9,658.00.
d. $12,058.00.
e. None of the above.

_____7.    The net income for the month of January is:

a. $1,675.00.
b. $1,193.00.
c. $3,740.00.
d. $2,547.00.
e. None of the above.

_____8.    When you reset revenue, expense, and dividends account balances to zero, this is known as:

a. Adjusting entries.
b. General journal entries.
c.  Debits equaling credits.
d. Closing entries.
e. None of the above.

_____9. Which two reports do you refer to complete the closing entries?

    a. Balance Sheet and Income Statement.
    b. Unadjusted Trial Balance and Income Statement.
    c. Adjusted Trial Balance and Income Statement.
    d. You use just the unadjusted trial balance.
    e. None of the above.

_____10. The total debit and credit balance on your January 31, 20XX trial balance is:

    a. $9,658.00.
    b. $12,058.00 .
    c. $8,851.00.
    d. $15,802.00.
    e. None of the above.

**True/False.** Write T for True or F for false in the space provided.

_____11. You must complete Parts 1 - 4 before doing the work in Part 5.

_____12. You use the Make Journal Entry link to record transactions in the General Journal.

_____13. QuickBooks: Online Edition will allow you to submit entries that are out of balance.

_____14. Computer equipment has a five-year service life.

_____15. When you record and post closing entries, you are transferring the end-of-year balances in revenue, expense, and dividends accounts to the retained earnings account.

_____16. You click on "Submit" between each entry to post to the general ledger.

_____17. A good way to see if you have entered transactions, is to print a Trial Balance.

Text and screen variations may occur since web-based software products backup and upgrade automatically.

____18.     Once the accounting period is closed, you will not be able to access transactions recorded before December 31, 20XX.

____19.     Your adjusted trial balance and post-closing trial balance are always prepared on the same date.

____20.     After recording closing entries, you should print a post-closing trial balance.

**Exercise 5-1.**    Using the reports that you printed in Part 5, End-of-Quarter and End-of-Year Transactions, answer the following questions.

1.  At the end of the quarter, your business's accumulated depreciation for the equipment  is:                     _____

2.  The amount of accounts payable owed on January 1, 20XX is:                     _____

3.  The updated retained earnings account balance on January 1, 20XX is:                     _____

4.  On January 1, 20XX, your total fixed assets are:                     _____

5.  On January 1, 20XX, your total liabilities and equity are:

_____

**Exercise 5-2.**  Complete the following.

1.  Copy your January 1, 20XX balance sheet to Excel.  Use **Exercise 5-2-1** as the file name.  Print your Excel balance sheet.

2.  Copy your January 31, 20XX balance sheet to Excel.  Use **Exercise 5-2-2** as the file name.  Print your Excel balance sheet.

## PART 5 INDEX

# 6 Advanced Features

In Part 6 of *Computer Accounting Essentials Using QuickBooks: Online Edition*, you use QuickBooks: Online Edition's memorize report feature, customize report feature, copy report data to a spreadsheet program and produce graphs, and use the activity log.

**SOFTWARE OBJECTIVES: In Part 6, you use the software to:**

1. Memorize reports.
2. Customize reports.
3. Create graphs.
4. Access activity log.
5. Complete activities for Part 6, Advanced Features.

**WEB OBJECTIVES: In Part 6, you use the Internet to:**

1. Access the Computer Accounting Essentials web site at www.mhhe.com/yachtessentials2e to check for updates.
2. Log in to your QuickBooks: Online Edition account.
3. Access QuickBooks: Online Edition's help feature.
4. Complete Internet activities.

**COMPUTER ACCOUNTING ESSENTIALS WEB SITE**

Before you begin your work in Part 6, Advanced Features, access the Computer Accounting Essentials web site at www.mhhe.com/yachtessentials2e. Software and book updates will be shown. Check this web site regularly for reference and study.

## GETTING STARTED

Follow these steps to start QuickBooks: Online Edition. You *must* complete Parts 1, 2, 3, 4, and 5, pages 3 – 167, before starting Part 6, Advanced Features. *The exercises at the end of each part must be completed, too.*

1. Start your Internet browser and log in to QuickBooks: Online Edition in the usual way.

2. Move your mouse over "Reports" on the QuickBooks: Online Edition menu bar. When the drop-down screen appears, click on <u>Balance Sheet</u>.

3. When the "Balance Sheet" screen appears, click on <u>Customize</u> in the upper center of the screen.

4. The "Customize Balance Sheet Report" screen pops up asking for Transaction Date options and Rows/Columns options. For "Transaction Date," select "Custom." For "Rows/Columns," select "Total Only" for the date. Type 01/31/20XX for both the "From" and "To" dates.

5. Click on <u>Create</u>.

**XXXXXXX Service Corporation**
**Balance Sheet**
As of January 31, 2004

|  | Total |
|---|---|
| ASSETS |  |
| Current Assets |  |
| Bank Accounts |  |
| XXXXXXX Service Corporation | 5,045.00 |
| **Total Bank Accounts** | **$5,045.00** |
| Accounts Receivable |  |
| Accounts Receivable | 0.00 |
| **Total Accounts Receivable** | **$0.00** |
| Other Current Assets |  |
| Prepaid Insurance | 210.00 |
| **Total Other Current Assets** | **$210.00** |
| **Total Current Assets** | **$5,255.00** |
| Fixed Assets |  |
| Computer Equipment |  |
| Accumulated Depreciation | -2,400.00 |
| Original Cost | 6,000.00 |
| **Total Computer Equipment** | **$3,600.00** |
| **Total Fixed Assets** | **$3,600.00** |
| **TOTAL ASSETS** | **$8,855.00** |

Scroll down the screen to see the rest of your balance sheet. The year shown on your balance sheet may differ. Compare your balance sheet with the one shown on page 161.

## MEMORIZING REPORTS

On every Report screen there are five buttons in the upper left corner. These buttons allow you to print, email, excel, customize, or memorize a report. You have already used the "Print," "Email," and "Customize" buttons. Let's learn about the ⟨ ↺⁺ *Memorize...* ⟩ button. The "Memorize" button creates a link on your home page to the memorized report and retains its customization.

Follow these steps to memorize a report. The January 1, 20XX balance sheet should be displayed on your screen.

1. Display the report you want to memorize and click <u>Memorize</u>.

2. When the "Add Shortcut – Web Page Dialog" appears, give the report a descriptive name.

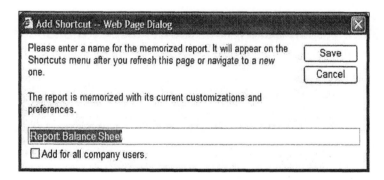

3. Click Save.

4. To verify that a link to the memorized report is on your home page, click 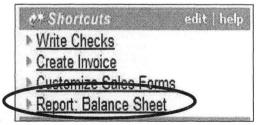. A shortcut to the report is now available on your home page. Later, if you want to change the

customization on a memorized report, you must memorize it again to save the changes.

## CUSTOMIZING REPORTS

QuickBooks: Online Edition has many different reports available for customization. Customizing reports gives you the flexibility to create the reports you want. You have three ways you can customize a report: display options, date options, and filter options. Let's look at the various types of reports you can customize.

### Reports

To learn more about the various reports you can customize, follow the following steps.

1. Move your mouse over "Reports" on the QuickBooks: Online Edition menu bar. When the drop-down menu appears, click on <u>All Reports (Report Overview)</u>.

2. When the "Report Overview" screen appears, place a check mark in the "Show Report Descriptions" box to display a brief description of each report if the descriptions are not displayed.

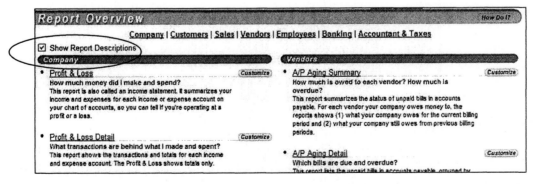

3. Scroll down the screen to read about each report.

4. When you have finished, click again on the check mark in the "Show Report Descriptions" box to hide the brief descriptions of each report.

5. Click on <u>home</u> to return to your home page.

**Customizing Options:  Display and Date**

In Parts 1-5 of *Computer Accounting Essentials Using QuickBooks: Online Edition*, you customized reports by selecting display and date options.  To review how to use these options, follow the following steps:

1.  Click your home page's memorized link to the January 1, 20XX Balance Sheet.

2.  When the balance sheet displays on your screen, click Customize.

3.  A "Customize Report-Web Page Dialog" box pops up asking about display and date options.

4.  For "Transaction Date" select "All Dates" (leave "From" and "To" blank), select "Accrual" for the "Accounting Method," and for "Columns" select "Total Only."

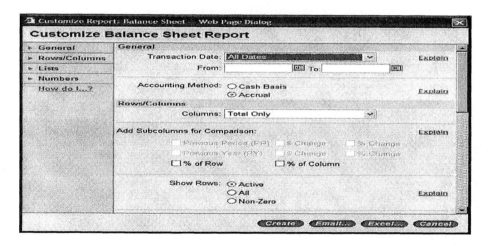

5.  Click on Create.

6.  A partial view of the customized report is shown below.

Scroll down the screen to see the rest of this customized balance sheet.

### Customizing Options: Filters

Follow these steps to filter report information.

1. Move your mouse over "Reports" on the QuickBooks: Online Edition menu bar. When the drop-down menu appears, click on <u>All Reports (Report Overview)</u>.

2. Click on <u>Transaction List by Customer</u>.

3. When the "Transaction List by Customer" report appears, click on the "Customize" button.

4. A "Customize Report: Transaction List by Customer—Web page Dialog" box appears asking for general, rows/columns, and date filter options.

5. In the "Transaction Date," select "All Dates."

6. Leave "From" and "To" date boxes blank.

7. For "Group By," select "Customer."

8. Compare your report to the one shown.

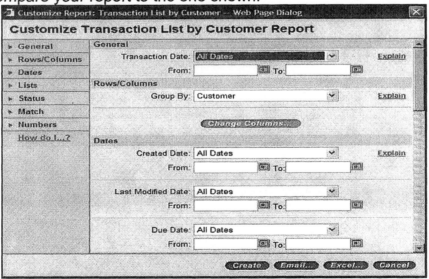

9. Click on the "Create" button.

10. A partial report is shown below.  To see the rest of the report, scroll down the screen or print it.  Your dates may differ.

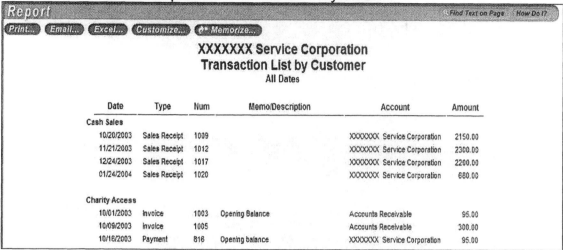

13. Return to the "All Reports (Report Overview)" screen.


## COPY REPORT TEXT TO A SPREADSHEET PROGRAM

You can copy the text of a report to any spreadsheet or word processing program.  Start with the "All Reports (Report Overview)" screen displayed on your screen.

1.  Link to the <u>Expenses by Vendor Summary</u> by clicking on it.

2.  Customize the report.  Select "All Dates" for "Dates," and leave blank the "From" and "To."  For the "Accounting Method", select "Accrual" and for "Columns" select  "Total Only."  Click on <u>Create</u>.

3.  When the report displays on your screen, click [Excel...] to view the report in an excel spreadsheet.

4.  Compare your spreadsheet to the one shown.

| | A | B |
|---|---|---|
| 1 | **XXXXXX Service Corporation** | |
| 2 | **Expenses by Vendor Summary** | |
| 3 | All Dates | |
| 4 | | |
| 5 | | Total |
| 6 | Big Bytes Supplies | 7,560.00 |
| 7 | Comtel | 1,121.00 |
| 8 | Jonathan Brent | 215.00 |
| 9 | Regional Utilities | 807.00 |
| 10 | Sales Products Supply | 2,580.00 |
| 11 | Santa Fe Rentals | 457.00 |
| 12 | Sun News | 270.00 |
| 13 | TOTAL | $ 13,010.00 |

## CUSTOMIZING GRAPHS

You can also display your report as a graph using your spreadsheet program's "Chart Wizard." Follow these steps to display your expense by vendor report as a graph.

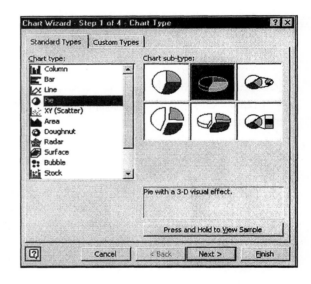

1.   With your mouse highlight the vendor names and amounts and click on the Chart Wizard icon on your toolbar ▥. *(Hint: See highlighted area in the previous screenshot.)*

2.   A series of "Chart Wizard" screens step you through the process of customizing your graph. In Step 1, select the chart type. Click on "Pie" and the "Pie with a 3-D visual effect" box. Click on "Next>."

---

3.   In Step 2, accept the "Data range" and "Series in columns." Click on "Next>."

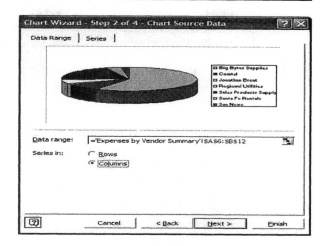

4.   In Step 3 set the title, legends and data labels. Click on the "Titles" tab. In the "Chart title" field, type: **XXXXXXX Service Corporation  Expenses by Vendor  October-January.**
     Click on the "Legend" tab. Make sure the "Show legend" box is checked and that the "Placement" radio button for "right" is selected.

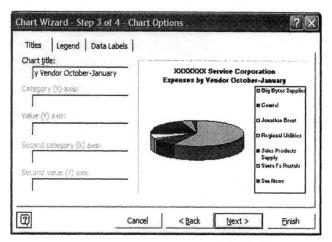

     Click on the "Data Labels" tab. In this last tab of Step 3, select the data labels for your graph. Select "Show percent" for the "Data labels" and also check the "Show leader lines" box. Observe that each vendor is shown as a percentage Click on "Next>."

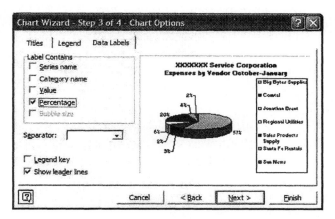

5. In Step 4 of the "Chart Wizard" place the graph "As object in:" your spreadsheet. Click "Finish."

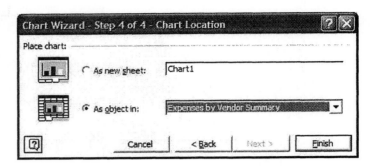

6. Move your graph around your spreadsheet until you are satisfied with its placement. Compare your spreadsheet and graph results to the report shown below.

7. Print your report and graph.

8. Save your report. For the file name, use "Part 6 graph."

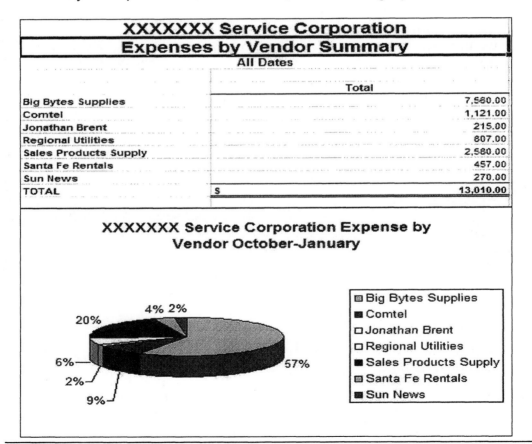

Text and screen variations may occur since web-based software products backup and upgrade automatically.

## CUSTOMIZATION

On the "Report Overview All Reports" screen, there many different types of reports to customize. You may want to select one or two of them to experiment with customization. For example, click on the <u>Profit & Loss Detail</u> report and customize it by selecting various display, date, and filter options. Remember, by accessing "Help," you can obtain specific information about a QuickBooks: Online Edition feature.

## ACTIVITY LOG

QuickBooks: Online Edition keeps a log of your activities while using the software. To access your "Activity Log," complete the following steps:

| Company | Custome |
|---|---|
| Home (Company Overview) | |
| Preferences | |
| Administer Company... | |
| Activity Log | |
| Budgets | |
| Chart of Accounts | |
| Recurring Template List | |
| All Lists (List Overview) | |

1.  Move your mouse over "Company" on the QuickBooks: Online Edition menu bar. When the drop-down menu appears, click on <u>Activity Log</u>.

2.  When the activity log appears, notice it displays the date and time of your most recent visits first. The log also displays the user and the activities engaged in while on your company site. A partial example of an Activity Log is shown below.

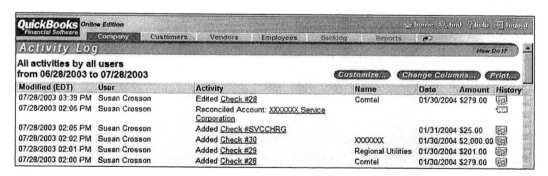

3.  Click on the "Customize button to see how the log can be customized.

4.  Print your "Activity Log."

5.  Log out or continue with the Check Your Progress activities.

The McGraw-Hill Companies, Inc., *Computer Accounting Essentials Using QuickBooks: Online Edition, 2e*

## CHECK YOUR PROGRESS

### Internet Homework

Start QuickBooks: Online Edition. Before logging in to your account, click on ▶See it work to view the QuickBooks: Online Edition videos and compare the various QuickBooks products.

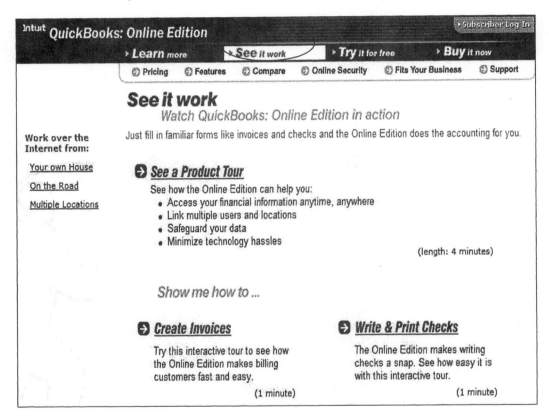

Complete the following questions after viewing a comparison of QuickBooks products.

---

1.  What products is QuickBooks selling?  How much does each product cost?

    _____

    _____

    _____

    _____

2.  Describe the types of free or risk free trial options each product offers.

    _____

    _____

    _____

    _____

3.  Which product has the most features?  Which one has the least?

    _____

    _____

    _____

4. What features does QuickBooks:  Online Edition have that the other CD-based products lack?

_____

_____

_____

5. List some features that would cause a company to switch from QuickBooks:  Online Edition to another QuickBooks software product.

_____

_____

_____

**Multiple-Choice.**  In the space provided, write the letter that best answers each question.

_____1.    To customize reports, you start by selecting which of the following QuickBooks:  Online Edition drop-down menus?

      a.  Company.
      b.  Vendors.
      c.  Banking.
      d.  Reports.
      e.  None of the above.

_____2.    The Computer Accounting Essentials web site is used to:

      a.  Log in to QuickBooks:  Online Edition.
      b.  Check software and book updates.
      c.  Complete Part 5, End-of-Year & Beginning-of-Year transactions.
      d.  All of the above.
      e.  None of the above.

_____3.    Why should you customize reports?

      a.  To display the income statement and balance sheet on your screen.
      b.  To display only the balance sheet on your screen.
      c.  To give you the flexibility to create the reports you need.
      d.  To change account balances on your reports.
      e.  All of the above.

_____4.    You can customize reports in what ways:

      a.  Change general options.
      b.  Choose row/column options.
      c.  Select list options.
      d.  Select number options.
      e.  A., B., C, and D.

_____5.   Which of the following is the date default when you display reports?

   a.  Current date.
   b.  Date of last transaction.
   c.  All dates.
   d.  Last day of the period.
   e.  None of the above.

_____6.   On the January 1, 20XX balance sheet, "Total Bank Accounts" is:

   a.  $8,485.00.
   b   $4,858.00.
   c.  $5,852.00.
   d.  $4,885.00.
   e.  None of the above.

_____7.   You link to the Sales by Product/Service Summary from the following report list:

   a.  Sales.
   b.  Customers.
   c.  Vendors.
   d.  Company.
   e.  None of the above.

_____8.   You can display the balance sheet by which of the following date criteria?

   a.  Fiscal year.
   b.  Last fiscal quarter to date.
   c.  This month to date.
   d.  Last fiscal quarter.
   e.  All of the above.

_____9.    Your Activity Log displays by the following date criteria.

   a. Fiscal year.
   b. Most recent activity first.
   c. This month to date.
   d. Calendar year.
   e. None of the above.

_____10.    In Part 6, Advanced Features, you make the selections for which of the following type of graph?

   a. Bar chart.
   b. Income summary.
   c. Expenses only graph.
   d. Pie chart.
   e. None of the above.

**True/False.** Write T for True or F for false in the space provided.

_____11.    You must complete Parts 1 - 5 before doing the work in Part 6.

_____12.    You use buttons in the upper part of your report screen to customize reports.

_____13.    You can copy the text of a report to any word processing program.

_____14.    The percentage of expense purchases from Big Bytes Supplies from October - January was 57%.

_____15.    The percentage of expense purchases from Regional Utilities from October - January was 20%.

_____16.    If you customize a memorized report, you need to click on "Memorize" to save the changes.

_____17.    The partial balance sheet shown on page 170 is the same as the balance sheet on page 161.

_____18.   QuickBooks:  Online Edition contains a graph feature.

_____19.   Check the www.mhhe.com/yachtessentials2e web site regularly for software or book updates.

_____20.   The work in Parts 1-6 is cumulative.

**Exercise 6-1.**   Using the reports that you printed in Part 6, Advanced Features, answer the following questions.

1.  On your expense by vendor graph, the percentage of Comtel is?                            _____

2.  On your expense by vendor graph, the percentage of Sun News is                            _____

3.  On your expense by vendor graph, the percentage of  Jonathan Brent is:                 _____

4.  On your expense by vendor graph, the percentage  of Santa Fe Rentals is:             _____

**Exercise 6-2.**  Complete the following.

1.   Print an "Expense by Vendor" graph pie chart for January 1 - 31, 20XX.

2.   Print an "Expense by Vendor" graph pie chart for October 1 - 31, 20XX.

3.   Print an "Expense by Vendor" graph pie chart for November 1 - 30, 20XX.

4.   Print an "Expense by Vendor" graph pie chart for December 1 - 31, 20XX.

**Exercise 6-3**.  Complete the chart that is shown below.

| 1. | October | November | December |
|---|---|---|---|
| Comtel | _____ | _____ | _____ |
| Sun News | _____ | _____ | _____ |
| Big Bytes Supplies | _____ | _____ | _____ |
| Jonathan Brent | _____ | _____ | _____ |
| Regional Utilities | _____ | _____ | _____ |
| Sales Products Supply | _____ | _____ | _____ |
| Santa Fe Rentals | _____ | _____ | _____ |

2.  Explain why November does not show a percentage for the vendor,
    Jonathan Brent.

    _____

    _____

    _____

    _____

    _____

    _____

## PART 6 INDEX

# Case Problem 1

In Case Problem 1, you complete two months of transactions for your business: February and March 20XX. You *must* complete Parts 1 - 5, pages 3 - 187, before starting Case Problem 1. The exercises at the end of each part must be completed, too.

In Case Problem 1, you will record transactions for the months of February and March; complete bank reconciliation for each month; and print financial statements.

If your instructor assigns Case Problem 2, you will complete the adjusting entries for the first quarter and print end-of-quarter reports. Case Problem 2 culminates the record keeping activities for your business.

Case Problem 3 is a student-designed project. You are instructed to write transactions for the next month (April 20XX) and complete the accounting cycle showing a net loss for your business.

Before you start entering transactions for February 20XX, let's look at the January 31, 20XX balance sheet. Make the appropriate selections to print your balance sheet for January 31, 20XX, and then compare it with the one shown in Part 5 on page 161.

## FEBRUARY TRANSACTIONS

| Date | Transactions |
|------|-------------|
| 2/02/20XX | Issued hand-written Check No. 31 to Santa Fe Rentals for equipment rental, $200. |
| 2/02/20XX | Received Invoice 145JE and a shipment of computer supplies from Big Bytes Supplies, Net 30, $1,725. |

| | |
|---|---|
| 2/03/20XX | Received Invoice EX133 and shipment from Sales Products Supply for the purchase of office supplies, Net 30, $245. |
| 2/08/20XX | Sold 50 hours of maintenance services on account to Two Sisters B & B, Invoice Net 30, $1,500. |
| 2/08/20XX | Sold 52 hours of maintenance services on account to Connections Cafe, Invoice Net 30, $1,560. |
| 2/11/20XX | Paid Big Bytes Supplies, Invoice 145JE, for the February 2 purchase, hand-written Check No. 32. |
| 2/11/20XX | Paid Sales Products Supply, Invoice EX133, for the February 3 purchase, hand-written Check No. 33. |
| 2/17/20XX | Received a check from Connections Cafe in payment of Invoice dated 2/08/20XX; Check No. 6201, $1,560. |
| 2/17/20XX | Received a check from Two Sisters B & B in payment of Invoice dated 2/08/20XX; Check No. 450, $1,500. |
| 2/24/20XX | Entered sales receipt for cash sales $2,420, received check No. 805 for 46 hours of repair services and 4 hours of maintenance services. |
| 2/28/20XX | Write Check No. 34 to Comtel for monthly telephone and Internet service, $236. |
| 2/28/20XX | Write Check No. 35 to Jonathan Brent for repairs, $220. |
| 2/28/20XX | Write Check No. 36 to Regional Utilities for monthly utilities bill, $235. |
| 2/28/20XX | Write Check No. 37 from checking account to pay dividends to sole stockholder, $1,500. |

## RECONCILE THE BANK STATEMENT:  FEBRUARY

Your business receives a bank statement every month for your regular checking account. The bank statement shows that checks and deposits have cleared the bank.  Use the bank statement below to complete account reconciliation for February.

| REGULAR CHECKING ACCOUNT February 1 - 28, 20XX | | | |
|---|---|---|---|
| Previous Balance | | $7,525.00 | |
| 3 Deposits (+) | | 5,480.00 | |
| 6 Checks (-) | | 4,650.00 | |
| Service Charges (-) | 2/28/XX | 25.00 | |
| **Ending Balance** | 2/28/XX | **$8,330.00** | |
| DEPOSITS | | | |
| | 2/20 | 1,560.00 | |
| | 2/20 | 1,500.00 | |
| | 2/27 | 2,420.00 | |
| CHECKS (Asterisk * indicates break in check number sequence) | | | |
| 2/1 | 28 | 279.00 | |
| 2/1 | 29 | 201.00 | |
| 2/5 | 30 | 2,000.00 | |
| 2/5 | 31 | 200.00 | |
| 2/15 | 32 | 1,725.00 | |
| 2/15 | 33 | 245.00 | |

From the "Banking" drop-down menu, go to the link for <u>Reconcile.</u> Complete the steps for reconciling your February bank statement.

## PRINT FEBRUARY REPORTS
Print the following reports for February 20XX.

1.  Print February's reconciliation summary.

2.  Print February's transaction list by date report.

3.  Print February's trial balance.

4.  Print February's balance sheet.

5.  Print February's income statement.

6.  Print January 1, 20XX-February 28, 20XX income statement.

## MARCH TRANSACTIONS

| Date | Transactions |
|------|--------------|
| *Date* | *Transactions* |

3/02/20XX   Write Check No. 38 to the Pro Insurance in payment of next quarter's insurance premiums, $210.

3/02/20XX   Received Invoice 190JE and shipment from Big Bytes Supplies for the purchase of computer supplies, Net 30, $1350.

3/03/20XX   Received Invoice EX203 and shipment from Sales Products Supply for the purchase of office supplies, Net 30, $195.

3/11/20XX   Paid Big Bytes Supplies, Invoice 190JE, for the March 2 purchase, Check No. 39.

3/11/20XX   Paid Sales Products Supply, Invoice EX203, for the March 3 purchase, Check No. 40.

3/24/20XX   Cash sales $3,280, received check No. 806 for 62 hours of repair services and 6 hours of maintenance services.

3/30/20XX   Write Check No. 41 to Comtel for monthly telephone and Internet service, $280.

3/30/20XX   Write Check No. 42 to Sun News for advertising, $80.

3/30/20XX   Write Check No. 43 to Regional Utilities for monthly utilities bill, $287.

3/30/20XX   Write Check No. 44 from checking account to pay dividends, $1,500.

3/30/20XX   Write check No. 45 to Jonathan Brent for repairs, $105.

## RECONCILE THE BANK STATEMENT:  MARCH

Your business receives a bank statement every month for your regular checking account. The bank statement shows that checks and deposits have cleared the bank.  Use the bank statement below to complete account reconciliation for March.

| REGULAR CHECKING ACCOUNT March 1 - 31, 20XX | | | |
|---|---|---|---|
| Previous Balance | | $8,330.00 | |
| 1 Deposits (+) | | 3,280.00 | |
| 7 Checks (-) | | 3,946.00 | |
| Service Charges (-) | 3/31/XX | 25.00 | |
| **Ending Balance** | 3/31/XX | **$7,639.00** | |
| DEPOSITS | | | |
| | 3/25 | 3,280.00 | |
| CHECKS (Asterisk * indicates break in check number sequence) | | | |
| 3/5 | 34 | 236.00 | |
| 3/5 | 35 | 220.00 | |
| 3/5 | 36 | 235.00 | |
| 3/9 | 37 | 1,500.00 | |
| 3/9 | 38 | 210.00 | |
| 3/21 | 39 | 1,350.00 | |
| 3/29 | 40 | 195.00 | |

From the "Banking" drop-down menu, go to the link for <u>Reconcile</u>. Complete the steps for reconciling your March bank statement.

## PRINT MARCH REPORTS

Print the following reports for March 20XX.

1.  Print March's reconciliation summary.

2.  Print March's transaction detail report.

3.  Print the March 31, 20XX unadjusted trial balance.

4.  Print the March balance sheet.

5.  Print the March income statement.

6.  Print January 1, 20XX to March 31, 20XX income statement.

| | Checklist of Printouts<br>Case Problem 1 |
|---|---|
| | February reconciliation summary |
| | February transaction list |
| | February trial balance |
| | February balance sheet |
| | February income statement |
| | March reconciliation summary |
| | March transaction list |
| | Unadjusted trial balance |
| | March balance sheet |
| | March income statement |

Name_____ Date_____

## CHECK YOUR PROGRESS, CASE PROBLEM 1

1.  On January 31, 20XX, what are your total assets?    _____

2.  How much is owed to vendors on February 28?    _____

3.  How much do customers owe on February 28?    _____

4.  What is the balance in your checking account on February 28 after doing the bank reconciliation?    _____

5.  Does the February 28 income statement show a net income or a net loss?    _____

6.  Does the March 31 income statement show a net income or a net loss?    _____

7.  How much is owed to the Pro Insurance on March 31?    _____

8.  What is the balance in the dividends account on March 31?    _____

9.  What is the balance in your checking account on March 31?    _____

10.  What are the cost of computer supplies on March 31?    _____

11.  What is the amount of bank service charges for the first quarter of the year?    _____

12.  Was any accounts payable incurred during the month of March?  (Circle your answer.)    YES    NO

# Case Problem 2

In Case Problem 2, you complete first quarter adjusting entries and print end-of-quarter reports. Case Problem 2 culminates the record keeping activities for your corporation.

If your instructor assigns Case Problem 3, the Student-Designed Project, you will have an opportunity to write transactions for the next month and complete the accounting cycle showing a net loss for your corporation.

## END-OF-QUARTER ADJUSTING ENTRIES

Record the following adjusting entries in the general journal (*Hint: "Make Journal Entry" under Banking.*).

| Date | Adjusting Entries |
|---|---|
| 3/31/20XX | Depreciation on computer equipment, $300.00. (Adjust 1) |
| 3/31/20XX | Insurance expired $210.00. (Adjust 2) |

## PRINT END-OF-QUARTER REPORTS

1. Print the March 31, 20XX transaction list with splits report.

2. Print the March 31, 20XX adjusted trial balance.

3. Print March's income statement.

4. Print a January 1 through March 31, 20XX income statement.

5. Print March's balance sheet.

6. Print the January 1 through March 31, 20XX general ledger.

| | Checklist of Printouts<br>Case Problem 2 |
|---|---|
| | March 31, 20XX transaction list by day report |
| | Adjusted trial balance for March 31, 20XX |
| | March 1 - 31, 20XX income statement |
| | January 1 - March 31, 20XX income statement |
| | March 1 - 31, 20XX balance sheet |
| | January 1 through March 1 - 31, 20XX general ledger |

Name_____ Date_____

## CHECK YOUR PROGRESS, CASE PROBLEM 2

1.   On March 31, 20XX, what is the balance in
2.   prepaid insurance?                                     _____

3.   How much is owed to vendors on March 31?              _____

4.   How much do customers owe on March 31?               _____

5.   What is the balance in your checking account on
     March 31?                                             _____

5.   Does the March 1 - 31, 20XX income statement
     show a net income or a net loss?                      _____

6.   Does the end-of-quarter income statement
     show a net income or a net loss?                      _____

7.   At the end of the quarter, what is the total amount
     of depreciation accumulated on your business'
     equipment?                                            _____

8.   At the end of the quarter, what is the total amount
     of repairs?                                           _____

9.   At the end of the quarter, what is the total amount
     of advertising?                                       _____

10.  What is the total amount of fixed assets
     on March 31?                                          _____

11.  At the end of the quarter, what is the total amount
     of net income?                                        _____

12.  At the end of the quarter, what is the total amount
     of utilities expense?                                 _____

# Case Problem 3

You have completed the record keeping for a service business in Parts 1 through 6 and Case Problems 1 and 2. It is the purpose of Case Problem 3, to have you write the next month's transactions for your business. Your transactions should be written so that your business shows a net loss. Include a bank statement at the end of the month so that you can complete reconciliation.

The chart that follows shows the printouts that you should have after your have completed recording transactions for one month.

| Checklist of Printouts Case Problem 3 | |
|---|---|
| | April reconciliation summary |
| | April transaction list |
| | April trial balance |
| | April income statement |
| | April balance sheet |
| | April general ledger |

Good luck! It is your turn to create the transactions for another month and complete the accounting cycle using QuickBooks: Online Edition.

# Glossary

**Accounts payable**    Money the business owes suppliers or vendors.  (p. 65)

**Accounts payable transactions**    Purchases of assets or expenses incurred on credit from vendors. (p. 65)

**Accounts receivable**    Money owed by customers to the business.  (p. 55)

**Accounts receivable transactions**    Credit transactions from customers.  (p. 55)

**Balance sheet**    A balance sheet is a list of assets, liabilities, and capital of a business as of a specific date. (p. 39)

**Browser**    The software used on a computer to connect and display information from a web site called a server.  (p.1)

**Chart of accounts**    A list of all the accounts used by a company. (p. 28)

The McGraw-Hill Companies, Inc., *Computer Accounting Essentials Using QuickBooks: Online Edition, 2e*

**Closing entries**

The purpose of closing entries is to reset revenue, expense, and dividend account balances to zero. When you record and post closing entries, you are transferring the end-of-year (or end-of-period) balances for the revenue, expense, and dividend accounts to retained earnings account.
(p. 151)

**Defaults**

Information or commands that the software or operating system automatically uses. QuickBooks: Online Edition refers to defaults as preferences.
(p. 54)

**General journal**

The general journal shows the debits and credits of transactions and can be used to record any type of transaction. For purposes of this book, you use the general journal to record adjusting and closing entries. (p. 145)

| | |
|---|---|
| **Income statement** | An income statement is where a business reports its revenues and expenses and determines its net income or loss for the period.  QuickBooks: Online Edition refers to the income statement as the "Profit & Loss" statement. (p. 149) |
| **Integrated Services**<br><br>**Digital Network  (ISDN)** | Faster connections to the Internet are possible using an ISDN line.  An ISDN line is a digital network that provides faster transmission of voice, video, and text.  (p. 2) |
| **Internet** | The worldwide electronic communication network that allows for the sharing of information. The Internet is also called the World Wide Web (WWW) or Web. (p. 1) |
| **Internet Service**<br><br>**Provider (ISP)** | ISPs can be companies such as America OnLine (AOL), CompuServe, Earthlink, or local providers. Usually for a monthly charge, these companies provide a connection to the email and the Internet. (p. 1) |

| | |
|---|---|
| **Items of service** | The various types of services that service business offer to their customers. (p. 62) |
| **Modem** | An abbreviation of MOdulator/DEModulator. A device that translates the digital signals from your computer into analog signals that can travel over telephone lines. (p. 1) |
| **Vendors** | This term refers to businesses that offer credit for assets purchased or expenses incurred. (p. 65) |

# Index

The McGraw-Hill Companies, Inc., *Computer Accounting Essentials Using QuickBooks: Online Edition, 2e*

The McGraw-Hill Companies, Inc., *Computer Accounting Essentials Using QuickBooks: Online Edition, 2e*